A TRIAD OF ANOTHER KIND

A TRIAD OF ANOTHER KIND
The United States, China, and Japan

Ming Zhang
Ronald N. Montaperto

St. Martin's Press
New York

A TRIAD OF ANOTHER KIND

Includes bibliographical references and index.

ISBN 0-312-21607-6

Library of Congress Cataloging-in-Publication Data

    1. United States—Relations—China. 2. China—Relations—United States.
3. United States—Relations—Japan. 4. Japan—Relations—United States.
5. China—Relations—Japan. 6. Japan—Relations—China. 7. United States—
Foreign relations—1993– I. Montaperto, Ronald N. II. Title.
E183.8.C5Z426   1999
327.73051—dc21   98–33859
                                                                                                                   CIP

Permissions:

Ming Zhang, "The Emerging Asia-Pacific Triangle," *Australian Journal of International Affairs*. Volume 52 No. 1 April 1998 pp. 47–62. Reprinted by permission of Carfax Publishing Limited, P.O. Box 25, Abington, Oxfordshire OX14 3UE, United Kingdom.

Ming Zhang, "The Taiwan Issue: A Text of Sino-US Relations," *Journal of Contemporary China*. Issue 9, Summer 1995. Reprinted by permission of the Journal of Contemporary China (JCC).

Ming Zhang, "TheAsia-Pacific Triangle and the U.S. Response," *Security Dialogue*. Volume 29 (1), 1998, pp. 126–128. Reprinted by permission of Sage Publications Ltd.

First edition: January, 1999

10   9   8   7   6   5   4   3   2   1

For Our Parents

Contents

Preface

Both scholars and policymakers would prefer a precise term for the time period they study. The last decade of the twentieth century, however, seems to continue its drift without a universal identity and is merely known as the "post-Cold War" era. This conceptual vagueness reflects the very complexity and uncertainty of current international relations. In the Asia-Pacific region, the old U.S.-Chinese-Soviet strategic triangle has vanished into history and, interestingly enough, the United States, China, and Japan seem to have emerged and formed a new power triad. Is this another hostile strategic triangle? How do the three great powers interact with one another? This new triangle appeals to many as theoretically challenging and politically pressing.

In fall 1994, we took up the present project at the Institute for National Strategic Studies (INSS) of the National Defense University (NDU) in Washington, D.C. We executed the study from an academic perspective and found it fascinating and exciting throughout the entire process. In 1995, Sino-Japanese relations deteriorated amid Japan's protests against China's nuclear weapons tests. In the same year, Sino-U.S. relations also plummeted after Taiwan's leader, Lee Teng-hui, was granted a visa to visit the United States. In 1996, a series of dramatic events seemed to finalize a dangerous triangular relationship: in March, the Chinese People's Liberation Army launched live-fire missile exercises around Taiwan and prompted the dispatch of the U.S. naval fleets toward the island area; in April, against the background of the Taiwan crisis, the United States and Japan held their summit in Tokyo; in September and October, China and Japan became entangled in a potential clash over the Diaoyu/Senkaku islands. However, a hostile triangle did not materialize.

By the end of 1996, the United States and China had already restored cabinet-level visits; in 1997, China and Japan held their summit. Most important, in late 1997, Chinese leader Jiang Zemin paid a state visit to the United States, the only such visit in 12 years; and U.S. president Bill Clinton visited China in June 1998, the first state visit by an American president in nine years.

We found the triangle hardly matched by a two-against-one model. Instead, we suggest that a reciprocal pattern is more accurate in describing the U.S.-China-Japan interaction. The findings themselves yield policy implications for decision makers to reckon with.

We are indebted to many friends and colleagues who have spent generous time and provided support for the book. Michael Stohl at Purdue University and John Freeman at University of Minnesota helped to refine the book proposal, and their comments are more than encouraging. Robert Sutter at Congressional Research Service, Masanori Nishi of Japan Defense Agency, and especially Masashi Nishihara at Japan's National Defense Academy offered much-needed insights into a final draft of this study.

Ming Zhang would like to thank Han Hua at Beijing University for arranging a seminar with her graduate students and colleagues; their criticisms and suggestions on the book are highly appreciated. Ideas and reactions from Ding Xinghao, Yang Jiemian, and Xia Liping at Shanghai Institute of International Studies, and Wu Xinbo and Ni Shixiong at Fudan University are likewise valuable and well taken by both Zhang and Montaperto.

Zhang is enormously grateful for the hosting institution INSS and the NDU Foundation, whose financial support made his visiting research fellowship possible. M. G. O'Connell, Tom Gallagher, and James Dugar of the foundation have proved themselves to be colleagues of understanding and enthusiasm to both co-authors. Among other sources, the Betac Corporation provided important initial funds for the project.

We also want to express our thanks to Karen Wolny at St. Martin's Press, whose editorial advice has smoothed the process from manuscript to book. Two anonymous reviewers offered both thoughtful and constructive comments for a final revision.

Parts of the book have appeared in various publications: chapter 2 (by Montaperto and Zhang) in *Journal of Contemporary China* (Colby College, Maine, No.9, Summer 1995, pp. 3–21), chapter 5 (by Zhang) in *Australian Journal of International Affairs* (April 1998), and parts of chapter 6 (by Zhang) in *Security Dialogue* (March 1998). We acknowledge the permission by the publishers for using these materials.

Finally, we want to thank our families. We dedicated this book to our parents for their many years' care of our lives and careers. Montaperto thanks each of his family members for their understanding and support of his work. Jiping Wu has, in every moment of Zhang's long journey, been ardently involved, and the newborn Oak W. Zhang has more than doubled the fruit of his research.

Ming Zhang
Ronald Montaperto
July 1998
Washington, D.C.

1

Introduction:
The Problem and Methodology

For nearly half a century after World War II, Sino-Soviet-U.S. strategic relations constituted a predominant power configuration in the Asia-Pacific region. In the 1950s, China and the Soviet Union maintained a close military alliance aimed at the Western bloc led by the United States. As the triangle evolved, the tension between the Soviet Union and the United States was more restrained than the conflict between China and the United States. In the 1960s, China confronted both the United States and the Soviet Union and even faced a potential joint attack by the two superpowers. The U.S.-Soviet relations went through a period of detente thanks to their arms control negotiations. In the 1970s and 1980s, the magnitude of the Soviet threat and the significance of the American power reshaped China's role in the strategic triangle. Whereas the Soviet Union and China found each other to be adversaries, the United States and China attempted a strategic partnership against the common enemy, the Soviet Union (Solomon 1982; Segal 1982; Medvedev 1986; Kim 1987; Zhu 1989; Ross 1993).

This great power triangle has, however, withered with the Cold War. Russia, still a geographic Asia-Pacific big power but entangled in domestic ordeals, has lost its past strategic assertiveness toward the region. The other two legs of the triangle—the United States and China—have consequently adjusted themselves to an unfamiliar political landscape in the Asia-Pacific region.

The East Asian Cold War history was not solely about the U.S.-Chinese-Soviet triangle. Japan had always been counted by the other three major powers as a potential military power. At the end of World War II, the United States occupied Japan. By the late 1940s and early 1950s when the U.S.-Soviet suspicion loomed up, the Chinese Communist Party established the new regime in Beijing; and when the Korean War broke out, the United States decided to sign a peace treaty with Japan and bring it into the U.S. security alliance system in East Asia (Zhang 1986).

In the 1950s, the United States encouraged Japan to build a defense force, and the rearmament alarmed the Chinese. But Japan and China did not return to a direct military clash; instead, the two governments sought to improve their relationship despite Tokyo's formal recognition of Taiwan. The Sino-Japanese relationship entered a brief period of tension in 1958 when Tokyo tried to create a closer military tie with the United States and Taiwan. China, in turn, launched a military attack at the offshore islands occupied by Taiwan and started a nuclear weapon program. Further, China saw the revision of the U.S.-Japan security treaty as a new scheme to project Japanese military power in Taiwan and Asia in general. In reality, Japan was becoming a unique major power which renounced war but gradually established a small and modernized military force (Barnett 1977).

Throughout the 1960s, China was extremely cautious in handling relations with Japan, considering its already deteriorating ties with both the Soviet Union and the United States. Tokyo likewise did not see benefits in provoking China and chose instead to be self-refrained. Japan's caution proved necessary when China and the United States reached rapprochement in 1972. In September, Beijing and Tokyo signed a communiqué to formally end the state of war between the two countries. In 1978, the two countries signed the Treaty of Peace and Friendship. For the next decade, Beijing perceived the moderate Japanese military power and the U.S.-Japan security alliance as favorable strategic elements against the Soviet threat. Tokyo was also relatively relaxed about China because of the U.S. military protection and the restraints imposed on China by the Sino-Soviet split (Iriye 1990).

What has struck people at the end of the twentieth century is the emergence of a new triad composed of China, Japan, and the United States. Scholars and analysts from these and other countries in the Asia-Pacific region have predicted and studied this new triad (Robinson 1988: 121;

Nishihara 1993: 85; Sutter 1994c: 1). Possibly having the old Sino-Soviet-U.S. triangle in mind, observers often portray the new triad in a fearful tone:

> Triangular relationships, by their nature, reduce international relations to a zero-sum game: any of the three powers is apt to suspect the other two of colluding to augment their bargaining power. A triangle made up of [China, Japan, and the United States] . . . could be a dangerous one (Funabashi 1993: 83).

The fear about this new triad comes from the change in the distribution of power among the new big three. As another author expounds:

> This region has begun to witness a new trend in which the United States as a superpower has been increasingly challenged by the predominantly regionally-oriented China, while Japan has become a great power in its own right with its new policy of shouldering more regional as well as international responsibilities. In the post–Cold War Asia-Pacific region, therefore, great power rivalry and manoeuvres are likely to become more intense (Sing 1994: 451).

Are we really facing a new hostile triad in the Asia-Pacific region? Must a triad be a dangerous one as some assume? In this book, we closely examine the nature of the Sino-Japanese-U.S. triad that has gradually emerged in the 1990s. In doing so, we are interested in what factors affect hostile and cooperative behaviors of the three countries. Our study also explores the pattern of the triadic behavior and how it will project in the future relationship. Thus, in this research, the nature and pattern of military behaviors by the three countries are the two key variables.

"A *triad* is a social system containing three related members in a persistent situation" (Caplow 1968: 1). "A 'strategic triangle' may be understood as a sort of transactional game among three players" (Dittmer 1983: 37). The literature on triadic studies can be analyzed in two parts. The first part is concerned with what determines a cooperative and hostile nature of a triad (Caplow 1968; Rapoport 1974; Ashley 1980; Dittmer 1983; Axelrod 1984; Goldstein and Freeman 1990). Individually or as a whole, the literature addresses perception, domestic influence, and international distribution of power, and their impact on behavior. The other body of literature focuses more on alignment and reciprocal patterns of triadic interaction (Caplow 1968; Rapoport 1974; Dittmer 1983; Axelrod 1984;

Hsiung 1985; Goldstein and Freeman 1990). The two parts of the literature are apparently interrelated and mutually supplemented.

In the first part of the literature, which is associated with the international relations literature in general, scholars consider the distribution of power as a determinant for the state behavior. According to Robert Gilpin, "the study of international political change must focus on the international system and especially on the efforts of political actors to change the international system in order to advance their own interests" (1981: 10). The distribution of power "constitutes the principal form of control in every international system" (29). Or, as others suggest, the balance of power is the key to understanding international relations and a worthy guide for determining policy (Haas 1953; Claude 1962; Waltz 1979). Overall, the literature highlights the impact of change in distribution of power on the nature of international behavior. Unfortunately, the literature as a whole is not decisive in what kind of distribution of power determines what kind of behavior. Kenneth Waltz (1979) and Robert Gilpin (1981) argued that bipolarity is more stable; Charles Kegley and Gregory Raymond (1992) found that the future of a pacific multipolar world is "equally plausible."

In this book, the distribution of power is an important independent condition on triadic cooperation or conflict. We observe, for example, how the growing Chinese and Japanese power has changed the balance of power between themselves and the United States and how this change has affected their behavior within the triad.

Literature and policy, adopting this way of thinking, have posited that the rising power of China and Japan constitutes both a long-term danger to Asia-Pacific security and a threat to U.S. national interests (Roy 1994; Betts 1993/94). As the foregoing literature review indicates, however, an international level of analysis is indecisive and inadequate in accounting for a country's behavior. We need to carefully examine whether capabilities (the distribution of power) are necessarily equal to threat. To a large extent, whether a state uses military force depends upon state leaders' perceptions about other states and upon their own national interests (see Baldwin 1993). Thus, we turn to the perceptional role in shaping a state's behavior.

Psychologists distinguish between perception, image, attitude, and expectation; in this study, we treat these psychological and attitudinal factors as a single subjective variable, "perception." Robert Jervis (1976) and Glenn Snyder and Paul Diesing (1977) suggest that psychological images of another country are fundamental determinants in choosing cooperative or hostile initiatives. There are hard-liners who are "conflict-ridden" and soft-liners who see more ground for common interests and accommodation (Snyder and Diesing 1977: 298–303). The former expect aggressive responses from the opponent and are therefore inclined to take firm actions. The latter believe that firmness will provoke stronger resistance and result in an escalation of conflict; concessions may win the enemy over (307–309).

In this study, we limit perceptions to those of state leaders. According to Alexander George (1969); Ole Holsti, P. T. Hopmann, and J. D. Sullivan (1973); and others, elite perceptions have a vital role in state behavior. "Cognitions are part of the proximate cause of the relevant behavior" (Jervis 1976: 28); diagnostic and choice propensities are two channels by which perceptions and attitudes may affect decision making (George 1979: 103). The available literature (Herrmann 1988: 183; Blum 1993: 375–376; Kacowicz 1994) has included the following important components for a belief system that explains why a government continues or changes its behavior over time:

(1) perception of threat from another country;
(2) perception of the international system as harmonious or hostile;
(3) perception of vital national interests;
(4) perception of capability relationships; and
(5) expectation for use of force or peaceful means.

In this book, we study whether state elite perceptions are "soft" or "hard" and how perception affects behavior within the triad. Thus, in addition to the distribution of power, we examine perception as an independent variable on state behavior.

Still, the neorealist system/power focus is criticized as incomplete and insufficient in explaining the dynamics of behavior. Critics cite domestic characteristics as a constraint on a state's military behavior, and thus as a vital determinant in its propensity for international conflict or cooperation (Rosecrance and Stein 1993; Bueno de Mesquita and Lalman 1992; Gourevitch 1978; Katzenstein 1978; Hermann and Hermann 1989; Putnam 1988).

There are two basic approaches to the relationship between domestic situation and international behavior. The first is the regime-structure approach, which is seen primarily in the literature of democracy and war studies. Proponents argue that democratic regimes, compared to authoritarian ones, are less likely to initiate war or resort to military force in the settlement of international disputes (Benoit 1996; Lake 1992; Rummel 1983; Zinnes 1980).

The other is the statist approach (Lamborn 1991; Levy 1989; Rosecrance and Stein 1993; Snyder 1991; Vasquez 1993; Hagan 1993). Statist researchers argue that the type of leadership and its orientation to foreign affairs define the state's foreign behavior; "who governs matters because it is normally a small elite who make choices related to going to war" (Hagan 1994, 184). Leader orientations and domestic constraints are not readily inferred from, or exclusively associated with, a certain type of political regime. Cooperative policy can also be favored by an authoritarian regime. The emergence of a hard-line leadership, instead, is the principal domestic prerequisite for war (Vasquez 1993). In addition, a state's "strength" or "weakness" in relationship to the society is central to explaining the state's foreign behavior. Weak states are driven by society—public opinion, interest groups, parliament, and the like. Strong states are relatively more independent of societal demands and pressures, and are more decisive in taking actions (Katzenstein 1978; Krasner 1978).

Thus, we need to take into account at least two domestic elements: (1) the type of leadership and its orientation (soft or hard) to foreign affairs; and (2) the strength of the state vis-à-vis the society. Empirical studies have indicated that when a state is constrained domestically by both political and economic conditions, that state will not take hostile international actions (Rosecrance and Stein 1993: 20).

In general, we adopt a three-level analysis of the dynamics for state behavior within the Sino-Japanese-U.S. triad. We consequently analyze elite perception, domestic situation, and the international (distribution of) power of each country to explore how these factors influence each state's behavior.

The study of the triadic nature (hostile or cooperative behavior) is one purpose of this research. The second goal is to unveil the behavioral pattern of the triadic interaction. The question is how the three major powers interact with one another over important issues. Theodore Caplow's work presents eight types of triads based on the distribution of power (1968: 6). He states:

> The most significant property of the triad is its tendency to divide into a coalition of two members against the third. The appearance of particular coalitions can be predicted with considerable accuracy if the relative power of the three members be known (1968: 2).

Caplow's typology has spurred a spate of research on triangular relations (Hsiung 1985; Kim 1987; Chen 1992) but has been challenged by other studies as well. Anatol Rapoport argues that "the interests of participants partially conflict and partially coincide" in n-person games and emphasizes that players "may be able to get jointly more if they coordinate their strategies" (1974: 2, 4). In other words, states are not in a constant power struggle. Based on this and other assumptions, the empirical study of the Sino-Soviet-U.S. triangle by Joshua Goldstein and John Freeman offers us an important approach to triadic behavior:

> These results—specifically the norm of bilateral reciprocity we find—imply that in general, strategies using cooperative initiatives elicit like responses in the real world of great power politics. . . . Hostile initiatives, however, . . . tend to fail, eliciting hostile responses (1990: 4).

In reality, however, these approaches do not seem to readily fit in explaining Sino-Japanese-U.S. relations, partly because this triad has not fully developed or does not provide enough evidence for a comprehensive or quantitative study. Caplow's theory would make no great difference in describing the formation of a U.S.-Japan alliance within the triad because the bilateral alliance was almost 40 years older than the triad. The triad has emerged in the 1990s but the time length is still too short for Goldstein and Freeman's time series method. Nevertheless, Goldstein and Freeman's reciprocation argument appears well worth a new test.

In this project, we examine the reciprocity in the Sino-Japanese-U.S. triad by observing the pattern of behavioral interaction. In particular, we study *how one actor affects the interaction between the other two actors in the triad* through consecutive and seemingly related events. In other words, each case study will indicate how one country affects the bilateral relationship between the other two countries. We then analyze *whether each country's behavior in later events reciprocates their counterparts' prior behaviors.* We thus take an inductive approach in this study and hope to provide more evidence on the triadic behavioral pattern. Differing from realist two-against-one alignment studies, our focus is reciprocation.

In sum, we first examine the nature of the triad via bilateral interaction through case studies. Chapters 2 through 4 apply three cases (the Taiwan issue in Sino-U.S. relations, the U.S.-Japan Security Alliance, and the China-Japan military balance) that should best expose the nature of the three pairs of bilateral relationships. In these three chapters, perception, domestic factor, and the distribution of power are examined in detail for their impact on bilateral relations. These chapters also sketch an overall picture of the triangular interaction. In chapter 5, we observe how the three powers reciprocate with one another and project their behavioral change in the future. For such a purpose, we focus on three events in 1996 (Japan vis-à-vis the Sino-U.S. confrontation during the Taiwan Straits crisis in March; China vis-à-vis the Clinton-Hashimoto summit in April; and the United States vis-à-vis the Chinese-Japanese dispute on the Diaoyu/Senkaku islands in September-October) that can best describe the action and reaction by each country. Finally, in chapter 6, we draw conclusions about the nature of the triad and its future behavioral pattern.

Our general findings are as follows. The nature of the strategic triangle is complex and evolving, but relatively stable. All pairs of bilateral relations are featured with uncertainties and yet no relationship within the triad can be characterized as hostile. Overall, the three powers prefer compromise to stalemate, cooperation to confrontation. As of the behavioral pattern of the triangle, the three powers have not pursued a two-against-one game; each power reciprocates other powers' previous behavior, positively or negatively; and all powers take measured and restrained action during the course of interaction. In short, the U.S.-China-Japan strategic triangle is different from a classic hostile triad: it is restrained and reciprocal.

We do not claim that this book is a comprehensive study of a Sino-Japanese-U.S. triangle. Nor do we attempt a major theoretical breakthrough. We simply apply some basic theories and methods to explore a new but important three-power configuration. Our hope would be fulfilled if our chosen approach explains the nature and projects the future of the strategic triangle, and if our analysis of triadic behavior offers new evidence for theoretical generalization.

2

Testing Sino-U.S. Relations: The Taiwan Issue

As commonly acknowledged, the Taiwan issue has been the most sensitive conundrum within the Sino-U.S. relationship. The communist regime founded the People's Republic of China (PRC) in 1949 after defeating the Nationalist government, which retreated to Taiwan. Since then, Taiwan has been a dramatic test of the development of China-U.S. relations. This chapter examines the extent to which the Taiwan issue has influenced the Sino-U.S. relationship and thereby evaluates the nature of Sino-U.S. relations at perceptional, domestic, and international (distribution of) power levels. Being aware of its existence since 1949, we concentrate on the Taiwan issue in the 1990s.

PERCEPTIONS

In this section, we consider how Chinese and American perceptions concerning the Taiwan issue continue to influence the Sino-U.S. relationship. How different are their perceptions and attitudes? What do these views tell us about congruence and dissonance within the Sino-U.S. relationship?

China

First of all, we need to point out that the Chinese view of Taiwan and the United States is part of its broader assessment of East Asian politics and security. In April 1997, China, Russia, Kazakhstan, Kyrgyzstan, and Tajikistan signed an agreement to reduce the armed forces on the borders. China called it a fine example for Asia-Pacific good-neighboring relations. By this model, all nations would develop a new security concept of equality and play down the role of military means in international affairs (Internet FBIS-CHI, Jan. 5, 1998). *Jiefangjun Bao* (Liberation Army Daily) elaborated new security as being political, economic, scientific and technological, and military, as well as social, which emphasizes equality and sovereignty. China warns that some countries are still obsessed with the "Cold War mentality," power politics, and military alliances (Internet FBIS-CHI, Jan. 17, 1998). In the eyes of the Chinese leaders, the United States is the military superpower in the post–Cold War era that influences China's greatest security interest, the reunification with Taiwan.

Chinese leaders' perception and attitude toward the Taiwan issue can be analyzed as a belief system that is most clearly embedded in the White Paper, "The Taiwan Question and Reunification of China," issued in August 1993 by the Taiwan Affairs Office & Information Office, State Council of the People's Republic of China. As acknowledged by the White Paper, Beijing's attitude toward Taiwan has been evolving since 1949, but has taken a turn since 1979, espousing peaceful reunification and "One Country Two Systems."

The first part of the Chinese belief system consists of peaceful intention. On January 1, 1979, China's National People's Congress pronounced its basic position as peaceful settlement of the Taiwan issue and called for talks to end the military confrontation between the two sides across the Taiwan Strait. On September 30, 1981, Ye Jianying, chairman of the Standing Committee of the National People's Congress, amplified the policy of peaceful reunification in his Nine-Point Proposal.[1] The following year, top Chinese leader Deng Xiaoping put forward the new concept of One Country Two Systems[2] for establishing a peaceful process of national reunification. In October 1992, President Jiang Zemin reiterated that Beijing would adhere to the principles of peaceful reunification and One Country Two Systems (*Beijing Review,* Sept. 6–12, 1993: v). Moreover, amid the Chinese leadership transition, Jiang declared his own Eight-Point Proposal in February 1995. He evoked a formal ending of hostile confrontation coupled with high-level visits between the two sides of the Taiwan Strait. Although he made no specific promise to withhold the use of force, Jiang emphasized that "Chinese do not fight Chinese" (*United Daily News,* Feb. 4, 1995: 1). After Deng's death and Hong Kong's return to China from the British colonial rule in 1997, China further highlighted its "One China Two Systems" policy toward Taiwan. Jiang said that Hong Kong's transition would "set an example for a smooth return of Macau and for the final settlement of the Taiwan question" (Internet New York Times, July 2, 1997).

Over time, Beijing's attitude toward Taiwan has tended to strive for peace. The slogan of "liberation of Taiwan" in the 1950s and 1960s has been gradually replaced by today's "peaceful settlement" of the Taiwan question. In this regard, Beijing wishes to use peaceful rather than military means to resolve the Taiwan issue. Beijing's intention coincides with official U.S. expectations of peace on the Taiwan issue. This will be discussed later in greater detail.

The second element comprising the Chinese belief system is its emphasis on Chinese sovereignty and legitimacy over Taiwan. To the Chinese in the mainland, there is only one China; Taiwan is a province or special administrative region of the People's Republic of China. "'Self-determination' for Taiwan is out of the question" (*Beijing Review,* Sept. 6–12, 1993: v). Accordingly, Chinese leaders believe that the Taiwan question is an internal affair of the PRC and that "it is the sacred right of each and every sovereign State . . . to safeguard national unity and territorial integrity" (*Beijing Review,* Sept. 6–12, 1993: i).

This statement is indicative of strong Chinese nationalism concerning the Taiwan issue. As the White Paper stated, "The history of Taiwan's development is imbued with the blood, sweat, and ingenuity of the Chinese people including the local ethnic minorities" (*Beijing Review,* Sept. 6–12, 1993: i–ii). A strong sense of nationalism also prevails among the ordinary mainland Chinese, including scholars and policy analysts. As they point out, modern Chinese history was made tragic by invasion, division, and humiliation; the Chinese across the Straits shared the torture and pain; and Taiwanese are also Chinese and it is not acceptable to separate Taiwan from China. National sovereignty, as these scholars conceive of it, is "absolute, universal, permanent, and indivisible" (*Renmin Ribao,* overseas, June 14, 1994: 3).

The paradox, as we see, lies in Beijing's increasing proclivity toward peaceful resolutions as seen against its ready determination to use force. The intention to use force constitutes the third part of the PRC belief system. In other words, the PRC acknowledges that the possibility of applying force over Taiwan persists and remains viable. Although the principles of peaceful reunification and One Country Two Systems can be explained as arguments for peace, the principles of sovereignty are transcendent and support the third part of the belief system that rationalizes and justifies the use of force. Beijing is straightforward in this regard:

> any sovereign state is entitled to use any means it deems necessary, including military ones, to uphold its sovereignty and territorial integrity. The Chinese government is under no obligation to undertake any commitment to any foreign power or people intending to split China as to what means it might use to handle its own domestic affairs (*Beijing Review*, Sept. 6–12, 1993: vi).

Thus, the rationale for using force remains within Beijing's belief system: China is a sovereign state; Taiwan is part of China; if Taiwan declares its independence, it is the right of the Chinese government to use any means to restore order and maintain national integrity.

We can assume that as long as Beijing's leaders hold such a belief system, the possibility of using force will stay alive. There is little chance that any Chinese leader will change this kind of attitude in the near future. In his February 1995 Eight-Point Proposal, Jiang clarified that China will not abandon its threat to use force over Taiwan, stating that forces of the PRC are aimed at countering foreign forces that attempt to effect Taiwan's independence (*United Daily News*, Feb. 4, 1995: 1). Visiting the U.S. National Defense University on December 10, 1996, Chinese defense minister Chi Haotian stated that "we hope to see a peaceful settlement yet refuse to renounce the use of force" (*The Pentagon Press Release*, Dec. 10, 1996). This confirmation has strong implications for Sino-U.S. relations.

The fourth element of the belief system is Chinese decision makers' and the public's perceptions of the United States with regard to the Taiwan issue. A policy paper by a group of government-related Chinese specialists in Beijing made a strong note about the sensitivity of the U.S. role:

> The Taiwan issue is the most sensitive issue in Sino-US relations. If handled improperly, it could bring about a confrontation between the two countries.
>
> The Taiwan Relation Act and American arms sales to Taiwan have been two ill wedges in Sino-US relations ever since the normalization of relations between the two countries. . . . we should pay close attention to the development of this issue, like whether Taiwan independence will or will not be put in the agenda of the Taiwan

regime in 1996 and how the issue of Taiwan's entering into the United Nations, . . . will develop (Panel 1994: 19).

Responding to the U.S. F-16 sale to Taiwan in 1992, Jiang Zemin commented: "Recently, the U.S. government is exerting pressure on us politically, economically, and in terms of foreign policy. It may do so for the time being, but it will not be able to continue this way in the future" (FBIS-CHI, May 24, 1993: 6). In his 1995 New Year's speech, Jiang again warned against "any forces that attempt to divide China" (*Renmin Ribao*, Jan. 2, 1995: 1). Referring to the United States, some scholars expressed their belief that if foreign countries support Taiwan's independence and separate it from the mainland, "China has no choice but to adopt all necessary means to protect its sacred sovereignty and will spare no blood and life in doing so" (Chen 1993: 249). The 1993 White Paper on the Taiwan issue stated:

> the U.S. Government is responsible for holding up the settlement of the Taiwan question. . . . [T]here are people in the U.S. who still do not want to see a reunified China. They have cooked up various pretexts and exerted influence to obstruct the settlement of the Taiwan question (*Beijing Review,* Sept. 6–12, 1993: iv).

Chinese public opinion echoes leaders' attitudes that the United States is hostile toward China. The public openly complains about economic inflation, political corruption, and other social problems. Chinese, however, concur with government leaders on the Taiwan issue. The ordinary Chinese would display their distaste about foreign support of Taiwanese independence. In the wake of the Taiwan crisis in March 1996, two books appeared on China's list of best-sellers: *Zhongguo Keyi Shuo Bu* (China That Can Say No) and *Zhongmei Jiaoliang* (A Trial of Strength between China and the United States). Both vehemently criticized the U.S. Taiwan policy.

The Chinese government, however, is not entirely hopeless and hostile toward the United States over the Taiwan issue. As the White Paper continues, "The Chinese Government is convinced that the American and the Chinese peoples are friendly to each other." If both sides abide by the principles endorsed by their 1972, 1979, and 1982 communiqués, "it will not be difficult to settle the Taiwan question" (*Beijing Review,* Sept. 6–12, 1993: iv). Meeting U.S. secretary of state Warren Christopher, Jiang said that the two countries "should avoid issues of conflict and build mutual trust" (*Beijing Review,* Mar. 21–27, 1994: 7). On December 10, 1996, Chi Haotian said to the officers at the U.S. National Defense University that "I am confident that American people, having experienced the Civil War themselves, should and will understand the resolve and determination of the Chinese people to safeguard state unity and oppose national separation."

In short, the Taiwan issue has resulted in a critical yet still hopeful Chinese view about the United States. This view has tended to impede the bilateral relationship, yet has not shifted the overall mood to be hostile. To the Chinese leaders, Sino-U.S. relations encompass broader aspects, from economic exchange to military security, in Asia and in the world. The stability of the Sino-U.S. relationship serves fundamental Chinese national interests.

The Chinese perception of the United States over the Taiwan issue is composed of both negative and positive, hostile and peaceful elements. The Taiwan issue has alienated Beijing and Washington and could cause greater mutual distrust. In this regard, China perceives the United States as a potential enemy. Chinese leaders, however, simultaneously display their restraint and maintain their peaceful intentions. The high sensitivity of the Taiwan issue has not resulted in an explosive Chinese attitude toward the United States.

The Chinese are ambivalent and suspicious about the United States. This is important for future development of Sino-U.S. relations.

United States

The United States has great strategic interests in East Asia. U.S. defense secretary William Cohen once discussed two pillars of U.S. security strategy in the Asia-Pacific region. The first pillar is the U.S. network of alliances with Japan, Korea, Australia, Thailand, and the Philippines. Another pillar is the set of overlapping multilateral frameworks for discussion and cooperation. Towards China, the United States seeks a steady and sustained engagement (Cohen 1998).

The people in the United States perceive the Taiwan issue differently from the Chinese. Despite some overlap, we cannot apply the Chinese belief system to the United States. The latter does not see the Taiwan issue as its internal affair but as an important issue related to its national interests. The U.S. attitude is also more diversified and less straightforward due to its subtle position: it is caught between its interests on the mainland and its security commitment to Taiwan. In general, U.S. perceptions on the Taiwan issue are economic, political, and strategic.

Economic Interests.   The United States wishes to maintain economic ties with Taiwan. In American eyes, Taiwan has largely liberalized its economic system; privatized its major state-owned industries; opened its financial, insurance, and stock markets; encouraged foreign investment; and taken measures to meet the standards set by the former General Agreement on Tariffs and Trade (GATT) and the current World Trade Organization (WTO). By striving to meet standards as a free-market economy, Taiwan certainly falls within the category of important interests that the U.S. government must support. The United States has vigorously upheld its economic interests in Taiwan. This attitude was reflected in both the U.S.-PRC Joint Communiqué on the Establishment of Diplomatic Relations on January 1, 1979 (see U.S. Government 1978) and the U.S.-China Joint Communiqué in 1982. In the 1982 joint communiqué, the two sides agreed that "the people of the United States would continue to maintain cultural, commercial, and other unofficial relations with the people of Taiwan" (*Beijing Review,* Aug. 23, 1982: 14).

Supporting Taiwan's economic prosperity and maintaining U.S.-Taiwan economic relations have been a consistent and fundamental policy of all U.S. administrations. Furthermore, as implied by the above two documents, U.S. non-official economic approaches toward Taiwan are also accepted by the Beijing government. In this regard, the U.S. intentions and interests do not necessarily pose a threat to Beijing.

Political Interests.   The United States tends to support Taiwan's democracy. Since the mid-1980s, the ruling Nationalist Party (Kuomingtang or KMT) has gradually relaxed its control over society in Taiwan. The emergence of the first opposition party, the Democratic Progressive Party (DPP), forced the government into further political reforms. On July 15, 1987, Taiwan's leader Chiang Ching-kuo lifted martial law, which also ended the ban on organizing new political parties. When Chiang passed away on January 13, 1988, Lee Teng-hui succeeded to the presidency and adopted a reform plan. Within a few years, bans on demonstrations, public rallies, opposition publications, and travel to the mainland were abolished. In April 1991, the "Period of Mobilization for the Suppression of Communist Rebellion" was terminated. In December 1991, the National Assembly election was held. The KMT won a decisive victory over the DPP; the KMT received 71.17 percent of the popular vote and 179 seats while the DPP won 23.94 percent of the vote and 41 seats (see Chiu 1994). In late 1994, Taiwan successfully held its provincial, mayoral, and lower-level elections. The DPP won the mayorship of Taipei, but the KMT still controlled governorship of Taiwan and mayorships of other major cities. In

March 1996, Taiwan held its first general election and Lee Teng-hui became the leader of Taiwan. As democracy develops in Taiwan, the trend of independence also grows strong. National Development Conference Resolutions adopted at the December 1996 convention states that both sides of the Taiwan Strait are "co-equal political entities," that "Taiwan is not part of the 'People's Republic of China,'" and that Taiwan opposes the theme of One Country Two Systems (NDCS 1997: 15, 21). Perhaps conceiving the U.S. support, Lee Teng-hui told a reporter in November 1997 that Taiwan "is an independent country" (*United Daily News,* Nov. 11, 1997: 2).

   Taiwan's democracy trends and improved human rights records serve U.S. political interests. The U.S. government recognizes the One China principle and accepts the Beijing government as the legitimate representative of China. As a result, the U.S. government has no official relations with the Taipei regime. The general U.S. national interests, however, endorse all democracies all over the world. So goes the White House paper: "Our long-term goal is a world in which each of the major powers is democratic, with many other nations joining the community of market democracies as well" (White House 1994: 20). China is not a democracy. The White House paper insists that "democracy and human rights are not occidental yearnings; they are universal yearnings and universal norms. We will continue to press for respect for human rights in countries as diverse as China and Burma" (24). Thus, we can assume that the U.S. government holds a more favorable political view of Taiwan over the PRC. The U.S. expectations are, perhaps, implied in such an argument: "The PRC must first come to grips with the reality of a democratic Taiwan. . . . When Beijing treats the elected government of Taiwan as an illegitimate entity ruling a renegade province, it insults the people of Taiwan . . . " (Munro 1994a: 120).

   However, even in the political realm, Washington does not want to treat China as a foe. "We are developing a broader engagement with the People's Republic of China that will encompass both our economic and strategic interests" (White House 1994: 24). "When considering how far to press principles like democracy and human rights in China . . . , Washington will need to carefully evaluate the risk that such efforts might damage relations with the country in question" (INSS 1995: 10). Assistant Secretary Winston Lord repeated in 1994 that the United States abides by not only the Taiwan Relations Act (TRA) but also its communiqués with the PRC. "It is up to the Chinese themselves to peacefully solve the Taiwan question" (*United Daily News,* Oct. 30, 1994: 1). Thus, the U.S. political sympathy with and support of Taiwan's democracy will not lead to its recognition of an independent Taiwan.

Under the principle of One China, Washington hopes to see democracy blossom in both parts of China. Furthermore, as pointed out by American scholars, democracy decisions "might not always be in the U.S. interests" (Lasater 1993: 248). For instance, if the people in Taiwan decided to be an independent republic and to completely separate from the mainland, they would precipitate a conflict across the Taiwan Strait. Consequently, the United States would find itself in an awkward position to "choose between principles of democracy and self-determination on the one hand and, on the other, the security and political interests concomitant to the preservation of friendly relations with Beijing" (Lasater 1993: 248). "A peaceful resolution of the differences between Beijing and Taipei, or even the perpetuation of the status quo, would be much more in the U.S. interest than to be drawn into a conflict with the PRC" (Clough 1993: 187).

Strategic Interests.   In the American view, the U.S. government is still committed to the defense of Taiwan's security and the military balance between Taiwan and mainland China. The 1979 TRA declared that the United States would consider any effort to determine the future of Taiwan by other than peaceful means as a threat to peace, security, and stability of the Western Pacific area and of grave concern to the United States; the United States would provide "arms of defensive character" to Taiwan; and the United States would maintain the capacity "to resist any resort to force or other forms of coercion that would jeopardize the security, or the social or economic system, of the people on Taiwan" (see the TRA text in Gibert and Carpenter 1989: 222–229). Thus, a potential conflict between the PRC and the United States does exist from this American perspective, and the United States may consider itself a balancer or deterrent against the mainland.

Nevertheless, the U.S. government would not readily go so far as to face a war with China. Neither the TRA nor the present U.S. strategy specifies how and by what military means the United States would get involved in a Taiwan Strait crisis. The U.S. military readiness to defend Taiwan is not on any urgent agenda. The bottom line for the United States is still peace and/or the status quo. At worst, we can assume that there is a potential for the United States to become somewhat involved in a mainland-Taiwan military conflict. At the same time, the U.S. interest is to promote regional stability by not fighting a war with China (Lord 1996: 151–154).

To compare the Chinese perception with that of the United States, the former perceive the United States as the source of conflict in the Taiwan issue: the United States has a history of violating its bilateral agreements, ignoring China's sovereignty, and supporting Taiwan's independence. The Chinese government reserves all means to achieve its national reunification, including a military attempt. On the contrary, the United States perceives its own strong national interests in Taiwan and advocates peace and stability across the Taiwan Strait. Washington believes that any military attempt by the mainland over Taiwan would constitute a source of danger and instability as well as international chaos in the Western Pacific.

Nevertheless, both the PRC and the United States agree to the One China principle, and both worry about the consequences of Taiwan's independence. Both the United States and the PRC advocate a peaceful resolution of the Taiwan question. In short, there is a potential confrontation between the two great powers, but the potential does not wipe out their mutual intentions of cooperation and reconciliation.

DOMESTIC INFLUENCE

We have shown in the previous section how Chinese and American perceptions can affect their bilateral relationship. In this section, we further explore the nature of Sino-U.S. relations through domestic factors pertaining to the Taiwan issue.

China

Corresponding to Chinese perceptions, China's domestic factors also provide strong dynamics for the settlement of the Taiwan issue. The first factor is China's shifting top leadership. Following Deng Xiaoping's ninetieth birthday in 1994, China essentially entered its Post-Deng era. It was widely acknowledged that Chinese leaders would maintain China's territorial integrity by all available means and fight any forces that support Taiwan's independence (Chen 1993: 249; Yi 1994: 684–685).

The Chinese Communist Party's (CCP) 15th Congress in September 1997 marked the emergence of the new leadership led by Jiang Zemin. In his Party Congress report, Jiang said that "we shall work for peaceful reunification, but we shall not undertake to renounce the use of force." He added that this was directed against the schemes of foreign forces to bring about the "independence of Taiwan." At the same time, Jiang emphasized that "on the premise that there is only one China, we are prepared to talk about any matter." He called on political negotiations between the two sides (*China Daily*, Sept. 13, 1997: 5). It is likely that Jiang's statements will serve as China's guidelines in the near future.

Chinese leadership correctly understands the significance of Taiwan for China and for the Beijing regime itself. However, as Kenneth Lieberthal points out, Chinese and American leaders seldom appreciate the internal factors that constrain their counterparts' decision making (Lieberthal 1997: 255). One-sided thinking would lead Beijing to a miscalculated strategy toward Taiwan.

A second domestic variable is the People's Liberation Army (PLA). The PLA does not pose itself as a predominant power player and rather is subject to the Chinese Communist Party-led political system. Nevertheless, the PLA makes a distinct unit within that system where it develops its own interests and even places significant influence on the top leadership. As it progresses in defense modernization, the PLA has emerged as a professional force that will certainly raise its own demands and exert its unique military power (Zhang Nov. 1997). On the Taiwan issue, in particular, the PLA's influence remains viable.

In the 1990s, the PLA demonstrated its influence over the Taiwan issue on several occasions. In early 1993, Deng Xiaoping led the reorganization of the Leading Group for Taiwan Affairs by adding more PLA representatives. After the U.S. decision to sell F-16 fighters to Taiwan in 1992, a large number of PLA generals urged the top leadership to get tough with Washington. Several times, senior military officers jointly wrote letters to Deng Xiaoping or Jiang Zemin, expressing their determination to confront the United States. From the PLA's viewpoint, the mainland China must increase relative capability to deter Taiwan from taking the road of "independence." Following the May 1995 U.S. announcement to issue Lee Teng-hui a visa to visit the United States, the PLA responded immediately. It abruptly cancelled all ongoing or scheduled visits to the United States. In July and August, the PLA conducted large-scale exercises targeted at Taiwan (Garver 1996).

A third domestic variable is China's economic development. China has developed strong economic ties with both Taiwan and the United States. According to Taiwan's official data, the two-way trade across the Strait has developed rapidly. From 1990 to 1993, mainland China's total trade with Taiwan rose by 4.6 times, of which the mainland's exports to Taiwan increased by an annual average of 1.4 times; imports to the PRC from Taiwan rose by an annual 60 percent. Mainland China shared 15 percent of Taiwan's total exports in 1993, whereas Taiwan took up only 2 percent of the mainland's exports market. This ratio indicates a greater economic flexibility enjoyed by the mainland over Taiwan in relation to their mutual exchanges (*United Daily News,* Dec. 25, 1994: 1). This kind of asymmetrical trade, however, may not favor a restrained military action on China's part. For instance, after Lee Teng-hui lobbied for a visa and visited the United States for the first time as a top Taiwanese official in June 1995, China took a series of hostile measures including military exercises against Taiwan. By June 1996, cross-Strait trade dropped dramatically. In the first quarter of 1996, indirect trade grew only 2.9 percent year-on-year, a sharp fall from the 40.8 percent year on year growth in the first quarter of 1995 (*China Trade Report,* Aug. 1996: 4).

Taiwan is somewhat cautious with regard to its rapid integration into the mainland's economy, whereas the mainland is pleased with the new trend. According to Beijing's statistics, primary export items from the mainland to Taiwan are raw agricultural materials, raw industrial materials, and semi-products. Exports from Taiwan to the mainland are high-level products including electronic equipment, chemical-fiber raw materials, and industrial chemicals. Further, the mainland considers its trade deficit with Taiwan as a contribution to the latter's economic development. Beijing also is pleased to see that Taiwan has invested extensively in the mainland's economy (*Renmin Ribao,* overseas, Dec. 24, 1994: 1). Taiwan's investment in the mainland was US$1.1 billion in 1992, US$3.2 billion in 1993, US$3.4 billion in 1994, and US$3.2 billion in 1995 (*Far Eastern Economic Review,* Nov. 7, 1996: 91).

Although the mainland-Taiwan tie is not entirely bound by economic profits, neither side wants to halt further economic integration. Total volume of cross-strait trade in 1996 reached US$22.208 billion, a growth of 5.8 percent over the previous year. The amount accounts for 10.2 percent of Taiwan's foreign trade, which divides into US$19.148 billion export and US$3.06 billion import for Taiwan (Internet FBIS-CHI, Mar. 3, 1997). Taiwan's investment companies simply dismissed their authorities' warnings about doing business in the mainland and continued to rush into the mainland's markets (*Far Eastern Economic Review,* Nov. 7, 1996: 90–91). In June 1996, as a breakthrough after the March crisis (see chap 5), Beijing permitted Taiwan's companies to invest in China's securities and futures industries.

In the same month, most significant to Taiwan's business, Hong Kong and Taiwan signed a five-year commercial aviation agreement that allows stopovers for flights between Taiwan and the mainland. This landmark air deal received Beijing's blessing and ensured that direct flights between Taiwan and the mainland began in early 1997 (*China Trade Report,*

Aug. 1996: 4, 6). On April 20, 1997, after decades of closure, the mainland Chinese cargo ship *Shengda* arrived in Taiwan's Gaoxiong port and reopened the shipping line across the Taiwan Strait (*United Daily News,* Apr. 20, 1997: 1). On April 24, the *Uni-Order,* a cargo vessel based in Taipei, became the first Taiwan-owned ship to legally make a crossing of the Taiwan Strait and embarked on a voyage to the port of Xiamen in mainland China's Fujian Province (Internet FBIS-CHI, Apr. 25, 1997; *United Daily News,* Apr. 25, 1997: 1).

Economic exchanges may push Beijing's policy toward Taiwan in a peaceful and constructive direction. Economic interdependence, if fully developed, may help the two sides solidify mutual understanding and appeal to compromise on more difficult issues (Zhang 1995). As long as Beijing makes peaceful gestures toward Taiwan, there is no reason for the United States to consider a military confrontation with China.

As we see, mainland China's domestic factors, ranging from the leadership, to the military, and to economics, are rather complicated and deserve an overall assessment. While the domestic situation sheds light on mainland-Taiwan and Sino-U.S. relations, it is especially difficult to foresee a future China. But it is the unpredictability that requires our cautious analysis. First of all, a political crisis in Beijing could press top leaders or the military for a violent solution of the Taiwan issue. This scenario would be more likely if Taiwan declared itself independent. In that case, the PLA's military action, coupled by its unstable leadership, would lead to a Sino-U.S. conflict. Yet, as the Chinese leadership has smoothly transferred to the next generation, a hostile action toward Taiwan seems to be remote. After the March 1998 National People's Congress, Jiang Zemin was reelected state president and chairman of the Central Military Commission. Zhu Rongji became premier, and Tang Jiaxuan foreign minister. The current leadership will be able to calmly handle its relations with Taiwan, at least in the near future. Meanwhile, Jiang and Zhu seem to be more willing than Deng Xiaoping or Li Peng to learn about American politics and decision making. This would also cast a positive influence on Sino-U.S. relations.

Moreover, greater economic interdependence across the Taiwan Strait may pose great constraints on both sides; it would be more costly for Beijing leaders to resort to force on the Taiwan issue. War would destroy the mainland's own modernization goals. Similarly, it would be a loss for Taiwan if it declared its independence. Besides damage from a war, Taiwan could lose the mainland's large market for its trade, investment, and national prosperity, as well as a chance for greater international status; after all, its reason to be independent. Thus, from the economic perspective alone, the PRC would pursue a more flexible policy toward Taiwan and the United States.

Yet, Taiwan's internal development could be the cause of Sino-U.S. conflict. As Taiwan continues its bid for independence, the anxiety in both the PRC and the United States could flame.

United States

There are even fewer integrated domestic factors in the United States that shape the U.S. policy toward Taiwan. The first notable factor is the U.S. Congress. On January 1, 1979, the United States switched its diplomatic recognition from Taipei to Beijing. Within a few months, however, Congress approved the TRA, granting legitimacy to the opening of unofficial relations with and defense commitment to Taiwan. In 1983, Senator Claiborne Pell secured passage in the Senate Foreign Relations Committee of a resolution endorsing self-determination for the people of Taiwan. On July 15, 1993, the Senate Foreign Relations Committee passed an amendment to the 1994–1995 State Department authorization bill that would amend the TRA to supersede any provision of the 1982 Sino-U.S. communiqué limiting U.S. arms sales to Taiwan. With a new legislation passed in 1994, the U.S. State Department, for the first time, received high-level officials from Taiwan. Therefore, it comes as no surprise that, to Beijing's thinking, the U.S. Congress is a hostile force against Sino-U.S. relations.

In 1995, the Republican Congress, led by Senate Majority Leader Bob Dole and House Speaker Newt Gingrich, took a tougher line toward China. Gingrich told Taiwanese reporters in Washington that "I've very strongly believed in the fact that there is one China with two sovereign governments who currently represent two different political entities" (*Washington Times*, Feb. 5, 1995: A8). The idea of One China and Two Governments has been vehemently criticized by the Beijing government. Gingrich also proclaimed his support of Taiwan's entrance into the United Nations. Jesse Helms, chairman of the Senate Foreign Relations Committee, was also known for his anti-Communist tradition and would not retreat from fighting "Red" China's human rights abuses (*Far Eastern Economic Review*, Jan. 19, 1995: 14–15). In May 1995, Congress pressed the White House to grant a visa to Lee Teng-hui to visit Cornell University. The incident caused a serious downturn of Sino-U.S. relations until November 1996.

There is another, even broader domestic force in support of Taiwan's interests. That is the American public.[3] They would like the United States to

- Back Taipei's position vis-à-vis the PRC in the UN and in other international organizations;
- Use the Taipei administration's preferred title, the "Republic of China";
- Supply weapons and support legislation advocating supplying weapons more advanced and in larger quantities (for example, 150 F-16s) than those recently supplied by the United States; and
- Firmly rebuff PRC efforts to obtain U.S. support for negotiations between the PRC and Taiwan (Sutter 1994a: 6–7).

The public voice creates a strong background for the U.S. Congress and even affects the administration's decision. In turn, pro-Taiwan legislations or government policies encourage and rekindle the pro-Taiwan movement. To the American public, Taiwan and China are two entirely different countries. Taiwan's products were once common elements of American daily needs; Taiwan is even enjoying greater prosperity and attracting more American tourists. To Americans, the PRC is nothing more than a communist state that has inflicted great pain on its own people.

American media and press are also receptive to the concept of Taiwan and the PRC as two countries. Academic journals aside, numerous think-tank and government-related publications, such as *Foreign Affairs, Strategic Review,* and *Washington Quarterly,* often invite Taiwan's officials to express their agenda for Taiwan's autonomy and higher status. Newspapers and magazines, including *The Washington Post* and *Time,* often highlight differences between Taiwan and the PRC and reserve pages supporting Taiwan's independence. As the Beijing-Washington tie turned from cold to mild in the end of 1996, for example, reports and commentaries in *The Washington Post* and *Washington Times* called the scheduled visits by Chinese defense and state heads "a bad idea" (*Washington Post,* Nov. 26, 1996: A15) and called attention to the human rights abuse in China (*Washington Times,* Dec. 11, 1996: A1). As a result, the freedom of the U.S. media and press creates another favorable force for Taiwan.

American business has a strong interest in both Taiwan and the mainland. The United States is Taiwan's main foreign investor and trading partner. The U.S. markets receive about 25 percent of Taiwan's exports while Taiwan receives a much smaller percentage of American exports. The U.S. trade deficit with Taiwan (US$8.85 billion in 1993) was the third largest behind Japan and China (Sutter 1994a: 1). Taiwan's US$80 billion foreign exchange reserves and its US$300 billion, six-year development program for the 1990s further attracted U.S. business attention. The U.S.-Taiwan economic tie, however, does not mean a decisive U.S. tilt toward Taiwan or an unfavorable gesture to the mainland. American officials and analysts believe that the United States should develop healthy economic ties with both Taiwan and mainland China (Sutter 1994b: 92). American business groups do not necessarily favor reunification of China or support an independent Taiwan. It appears that the interests of American businesses coincide with the U.S. government in terms of security and stability across the Taiwan Strait.

According to Chinese statistics, Sino-U.S. trade volume was US$2.45 billion in 1979 but rocketed to US$42.84 billion in 1996. The United States was China's third largest trade partner in 1979 and rose to the second in 1996. Among trade partners of the United States, China ranked twenty-forth in 1980 but climbed to fifth place in 1995. American investment in China also witnessed an extensive development. By the end of 1996, 22,240 projects with U.S. investment had been launched in China with a committed investment volume of US$35.17 billion. Excluding Hong Kong and Taiwan, the United States is the second largest investor in China, next to Japan (*China Daily,* Mar. 22, 1997: 4).

Still, the U.S. administration directly conducts foreign policy. Even though Congress and the public have left a clear imprint on the U.S. government policy toward China and U.S.-Taiwan relations, the U.S. government officially adheres to the One China principle, maintains global security and strategic cooperation with Beijing, and encourages Chinese to peacefully settle the Taiwan issue themselves. At the same time, the U.S. government would not fulfill its promises to reduce its arms sales to Taiwan in quality and quantity; instead, it has upgraded its official contacts with Taiwan (the U.S. secretary of transportation visited Taiwan in 1994) and continued to be pressed by domestic pro-Taiwan forces. However, few, at least in the U.S. government, desire to restore official relations with Taiwan. Many judge that a radical step toward Taiwan would upset the stability across the Taiwan Strait and lose China for a long time to come (Shambaugh 1995; Freeman et al. 1995; CQ Researcher 1996; Freeman 1996; Berger 1997).

In sum, the U.S. domestic factors exert great pressure on the official U.S. Taiwan policy. They are undercurrents beneath the Taiwan issue that could generate a new confrontation between the PRC and the United

States. If congressional and public opinion becomes the mainstream of U.S. Taiwan policymaking, the PRC-U.S. relationship is expected to erupt and decline. This possibility is, however, balanced by overall U.S. business interests and government policy. The official U.S. Taiwan policy does not entirely agree with Beijing and even draws Beijing's protests. But the United States and China find common ground in acknowledging the One China principle and working toward regional stability. In broader terms, Washington has been walking a cautious line in order to strike a balance between the two great powers.

MILITARY POWER ACROSS THE TAIWAN STRAIT

In the earlier two sections, we analyzed Chinese and American attitudes toward each other and their respective domestic influence on the Taiwan issue. In this section, we compare the Chinese and U.S. (through Taiwan) military power concerning a potential conflict over Taiwan in order to assess Sino-U.S. interaction.

A group of Chinese officers once analyzed the PLA capabilities in dealing with a Taiwan Strait crisis. In competing for air superiority, if Taiwan mobilizes 280 advanced third-generation warplanes (80 percent of its total air force), the PLA must employ at least 1,000 planes, including at least 400 J-8 fighters and about 600 bombers. At sea, the PLA navy must dispatch 750 warships, more than 100 landing craft, and 100,000 landing troops. Meanwhile, the mainland will have to "make best use" of its submarines (see Munro 1994b: 366). This is only one of the scenarios described by many analysts in the mainland, Taiwan, and the United States.

We begin with the mainland's military buildup to analyze the power distribution across the Strait. China's military modernization has achieved remarkable progress due to input from Russia and Israel. It is well known that mainland China has purchased Su-27 fighters, Kilo-Class submarines, and an S-300 air-defense missile system, as well as pertinent technology from Russia (Gill and Kim 1995: 68). In addition, Russian military technicians are helping upgrade China's military machine in several Chinese cities. Russia supplied 97 percent of China's US$1.75 billion in arms imports from 1992 to 1994 (*Far Eastern Economic Review,* Mar. 13, 1997: 20); or as of 1997, China had purchased US$5 billion to US$6 billion in Russian arms since 1991 (*Wall Street Journal,* Aug. 1, 1997: 11). The following is a purchase list.

1. Aircraft. China has purchased up to 72 Su-27 fighters, comparable to the U.S. F-15s, and secured a US$2.5 billion deal that would allow China to produce up to 200 more. Other possible deals might include Su-30MK long-range attack aircraft and the Il-78 air-refueling tanker, as well as aircraft equipped with an airborne early-warning and control system.
2. Submarines. Russia has sold China four Kilo-class conventional submarines. The first two are Type 877EKM models, which had been delivered as of 1997; the next two will be of the more advanced Type 636, and are expected to arrive in China by late 1998. The advanced version is about as quiet as the best U.S. nuclear-powered attack submarines.
3. Warships. China has purchased two Sovremenny-class destroyers, which will carry Sunburn supersonic missiles designed to attack aircraft carriers. This purchase was seen as a direct Chinese reaction to the March 1996 crisis in the Taiwan Strait (*Far Eastern Economic Review,* Mar. 13, 1997: 20; *Jane's Defense Weekly,* July 30, 1997: 16).

It also has become public that even before Russia and the former Soviet Union began arms sales, Israel had made significant contributions to the PLA development. Secret Sino-Israeli arms deals started as early as the late 1970s. China, one of the fastest-growing markets for the Israeli arms industry, purchased about US$3 billion of Israeli weapons over the 1984–94 period. The arms received by the PLA included electronic fire-control systems; anti-tank missiles; and, more importantly, high technology. Almost all Israeli arms-makers, such as IAI, Rafael, and EI-Op, have frequent connections with Chinese buyers. This sensitive cooperation has caused serious concerns and questioning by the U.S. government, which fears its own secret technology has been leaked to China through Israel (*Far Eastern Economic Review,* Jan. 19, 1995: 26–27).

As a result of foreign buying and self-development, the PLA has embarked on the road of gradual modernization. It has been reported for years that China is interested in purchasing or building aircraft carriers. Equipped with such weaponry, China would become more assertive toward Taiwan. The PLA navy has developed considerable new forces in the 1990s. The number of naval personnel has risen from 8 percent to 11 percent of the PLA's total whereas the ground forces have been reduced from 81 to 75 percent of the total (Klintworth 1997: 6). The navy has 61 submarines (including 1 Xia Class, 5 Han Class, 3 Kilo Class, 1 Song Class, and some Ming and Romeo Class), 18 destroyers (2 Lulu Type, 1

Luda III, 1 modified Luda, and 14 Luda Type-051), 36 frigates (4 Jiang-wei Type, 30 Jianghu Type, and 2 Chengdu Type), 830 patrol and coastal combatants, and 71 amphibious ships (*Military Balance* 1997/98: 177).

The air force has 100 H-6 medium bombers, 400 Q-5 fighter–ground-attack, and 2,748 fighters (most are old J-6; others include 500 J-7, 200 J-8, and less than 100 Su-27) (178). In addition, Super-7 and J-10, both incorporating foreign technology, will constitute a new generation of air force power, with more Su-27 by the year 2000 (Allen, Krumel, and Pollack 1995: 149–150, 155).

The PLA's missile systems have become increasingly advanced and comprehensive, ranging from DF-7 (180 km) to DF-18 (1000 km). These arms not only threaten Taiwan but also enjoy a broad consumer market in the Third World countries. Consequently, the PLA's arms sales worry the United States (Zhan 1994: 130–137). As of the mid-1990s, China's nuclear forces (the Second Artillery) has 50 DF-3 missiles, 20 DF-4 missiles, 20 DF-5 missiles, 36 DF-21 missiles, and 12 JL-1 missiles, with 450 nuclear warheads. China will continue to maintain a triad of nuclear forces (land-based missiles, bombers, and submarine-launched ballistic missiles), while land-based ballistic missiles will remain the mainstay of Chinese nuclear forces. Two mobile missile programs are at the late stage of development: the DF-31 and the DF-41. The DF-31 will be a three-stage missile capable of carrying a 700 kg payload over a range of 8,000 km and will be deployed in the late 1990s. The DF-41 is planned to be a mobile, three-stage, solid propellant Intercontinental Ballistic Missile (ICBM) with a range of 12,000 km and designed to replace the DF-5 in the first decade of the twenty-first century (Norris, Burrows, and Field-house 1994: 359, 372). Chinese missiles, especially those short-range M-9 missiles, could "diminish the strategic significance of Taiwan's heavily fortified islands of Jinmen and Mazu" (*Defense News,* Aug. 26–Sept. 1, 1996: 8).

According to a report, Beijing drafted a war plan against Taiwan. The plan made its assessment in view of the military strength across the Strait and the military action likely taken by the United States in the war. The plan was reportedly supported by many PLA generals (*Ming Pao,* Sept. 26, 1996: A14). It also was reported that the PLA has conducted sea-crossing offensive exercises and improved such capabilities. For example, an elite group army of the Guangzhou Military Region has been instructed in recent years to carry out "sea-crossing and landing opera-tions" projects, aimed at Taiwan. The report suggested that the PLA has achieved sea-crossing-related logistic, air fighting, and landing capabili-ties (*Kuang Chiao Ching,* July 16, 1997: 56–66). Another report argued that the PLA will have a sufficient number of vessels to ferry a massive force across the Strait, including civil ships. Meanwhile, the report suggested, the PLA could block the Taiwan Strait with small mines. This report also took into account the Japanese and American support of Taiwan during a possible war (*Kuang Chiao Ching*, Aug. 16, 1997: 78–83). Taiwan's defense chief Chiang Chung-lin emphatically told an American visitor that China is capable of invading Taiwan either by staging missile attacks or by employing a maritime blockade (FBIS-CHI, Mar. 6, 1998).

Nevertheless, in a balanced analysis, we cannot exaggerate China's military power in any extreme manner. As a report described, "China has rushed to buy sophisticated hardware, but often without upgrading training, maintenance or technical support accordingly." Two Kilo-class submarines and some Su-27 fighters broke down due to poor maintenance, according to this report (*Wall Street Journal*, Aug. 1, 1997: 1, 11). Similarly, as an author wrote, "to execute even basic maritime strategy—to defend the homeland, protect disputed territories in the East and South China Seas, and exploit maritime mineral resources—China has a navy of questionable effectiveness but unquestioned technological shortcomings" (Cole 1997: 37).

The mainland's military buildup certainly poses a threat to Taiwan; yet, it would be an exaggeration to say that the growth of military power is always equal to the increase of threat. In the 1990s, all Asian nations have upgraded their military capabilities. Further, in a mathematical sense, the advancement of Taiwan's weaponry may have reduced the mainland's threat. By the end of 1996, Western analysts tended to acknowledge that they might have exaggerated China threat based on its military power (see *New York Times*, Dec. 3, 1996: A1, A10).

Now let us look at Taiwan's military buildup. As China's military assertiveness was seen as increasing in the early 1990s, the United States felt compelled to revise its arms-sale policy to Taiwan. Assessing the changes between the mainland and Taiwan, the Bush administration decided to sell 150 F-16 A/Bs to Taiwan. "Because of the US decisions to sell F-16s, there is no more arms-sale containment policy," said Richard Yang of the Sun Yatsen Center for Policy Studies in Taiwan (*Far Eastern Economic Review*, Sept. 17, 1992: 12). Meanwhile, France sold Mirage 2000–5E fighters to Taiwan. Israel also made a good advance into Taiwan's arms market by co-producing missiles and missile boats. But the largest project, the 1992 $600 million contract for 40 IAI-made Kfir C7 jets, was terminated due to the combined pressure from the United States and China (*Far Eastern Economic Review*, Jan. 19, 1995: 27).

In August 1996, the U.S. Department of Defense endorsed a US$420 million sale of 1,299 Stinger anti-aircraft missiles and support equipment to Taiwan (*Defense News,* Aug. 26–Sept. 1, 1996: 2). American officials assured Taiwan of continued U.S. arms sales in the future abiding by the TRA (Internet FBIS-CHI, Sept. 6, 1996). In 1996, U.S. arms sales to Taiwan increased 121 percent over the previous year, reaching almost US$460 million and ranking ninth among all U.S. arms sales (*United Daily News,* Mar. 1, 1997: 1). One Chinese analyst argued that Taiwan is posing a genuine threat to mainland China as its F-16s can reach virtually any mainland city and its Perry-Class warships can make several round trips to any mainland port (Internet FBIS-CHI, Oct. 15, 1997). Meanwhile, however, U.S. officials want to assure that "U.S. sales do not upset such balances" between the two sides of the Chinese.[4]

In parallel with the military buildup in mainland China, Taiwan's military strength has reached a new height. The army has 240,000 personnel. Its main battle tanks include 100 M-48A5, 450 M-48H, and 160 M-60A3. Its light tanks include 230 M-24 and 675 M-41/Type 64. Armored personnel carriers include 650 M-113 and 300 V-150 commando. The army is also equipped with 970 towed artillery and other weapons (*Military Balance* 1996/97: 196–197).

The navy has 68,000 personnel, 4 submarines (2 Hailung, 2 Haishih), 36 principal surface combatants (18 destroyers and 18 frigates), 98 patrol and coastal combatants, 16 mine-warfare ships, and 21 amphibious ships (197).

By the year 2000, the air force will include 150 F-16, 60 mirage 2000–5, and 130 IDF. In addition, it will have 4 E-2T airborne warning and command (AWAC) aircraft (Lin 1996: 579–581).

Without a doubt, the distribution of power between mainland China and Taiwan should be considered an important factor for the regional situation. As one expert describes:

> With regard to the military balance between the PRC and Taiwan, Taiwan relies on quality of weaponry to offset a much more powerful adversary. In many categories, Taiwan's weapons inventory is qualitatively superior to the PRC's at present (particularly naval) and in the future (air). . . . Taiwan has its weaknesses—particularly in anti-submarine warfare and anti-ballistic missile defense—but in both cases [Taiwan] is moving to remedy the deficiencies (Shambaugh 1996: 1318).

Therefore, as military power continues to grow across the Taiwan Strait, the distribution of power has generally maintained its status quo. But the power status alone fails to explain what has happened across the Strait in the 1990s. For instance, U.S. arms sales to Taiwan could not prevent hostility across the Strait; despite the balance of power, perceptional and domestic factors caused high anxiety from Beijing. Ten years down the road, it is possible that China will become more powerful than Taiwan; in other words, military balance will become imbalance of power. Under that scenario, it becomes even more urgent to study how perception and politics will take part in the stability across the Taiwan Strait (Montaperto 1998). Now we turn to a fuller discussion of Sino-U.S. interaction.

SINO-U.S. INTERACTION

From the behavioral perspective, there is indeed evidence illustrating China's threat to Taiwan, and indirectly toward the United States. The PLA military exercises from 1994 to 1996 provide concrete explanations. The Sacred 1994 and East Sea 4 were two major unprecedented exercises jointly conducted by the PLA army, navy, and air force. Military analysts in Taipei believed that the PLA had beefed up its capabilities to obtain superiority in a future Strait crisis. The competence and excellence displayed in the power, speed, and collaboration of the two exercises impressed military officers in Taiwan (*United Daily News,* Jan. 9, 1995: 1). In the summer of 1995, the PLA opened several rounds of military exercises off Taiwan with air and naval missile firings in the East China Sea (*New York Times,* Aug. 19, 1995: A1, A6). Finally, in March 1996, the PLA's condensed drills led the tension across the Taiwan Strait into a crisis (see chap 5).

China's actions to fulfill its sovereignty promises have moved itself toward a potential military clash with both Taiwan and the United States. At the same time, however, Beijing also is wasting no time seeking nonviolent solutions. The F-16 case is an example. Chinese vice foreign minister Liu Huaqiu called this deal a "shock and outrage" and warned of retaliation (*Far Eastern Economic Review,* Sept. 17, 1992: 12). China immediately withdrew from the five-power talks on arms control. Other than that, however, Beijing did not take any direct counteraction. "Moreover, Beijing did not condemn Taiwan for the arms purchase; its behavior suggested strongly that it wanted to avoid any action that would interfere with the smooth development of economic and other interaction between the two sides of the Strait" (Clough 1993: 183).

After all, China seeks a peaceful rather than violent solution of the

Taiwan issue, and that strategy greatly depends on Taiwan's independence tendency. After 1996, Beijing tended to use diplomatic, economic, and other non-military means to either lure or press Taiwan. As one official article stated, "political issues in cross-strait relations should be resolved through political negotiations" (Internet FBIS-CHI, Sept. 10, 1997). In April 1998, Beijing and Taipei resumed middle-level official dialogues. We should not ignore the soft part of the Chinese behavior that may lead to a long journey of peaceful resolution. China's behavior over the Taiwan Strait directly affects its relations with the United States.

Away from the prospect of a perpetuated Sino-U.S. confrontation, the two military forces attempted dialogue and cooperation after the 1989 Tiananmen massacre, which marked a beginning of another period of fragile relationship. Evidence in this regard includes the agreements pertaining to the Missile Technology Control Regime (MTCR) and nuclear weapons material production signed by Secretary of State Warren Christopher and Foreign Minister Qian Qichen in late 1994 (*Renmin Ribao,* Oct. 6, 1994; *Far Eastern Economic Review,* Oct. 20, 1994: 20). In other fields, China supported the U.S.-North Korean Nuclear Agreement (*Washington Post,* Nov. 14, 1994: 1), and the two armies have frequently exchanged visits. In July 1996, Anthony Lake, U.S. national security advisor, visited Beijing and initiated the recovery of Sino-U.S. relations after Lee's visit to Cornell University in June 1995 (*Washington Post,* July 11, 1996: A21; *China Daily,* July 10, 1996: 1). In October 1996, the director of the U.S. Arms Control and Disarmament Agency (ACDA) John Holum visited Beijing and pledged to limit U.S. arms sales to Taiwan (*China Daily,* Oct. 11, 1996: 1). In late November, 1996 Secretary of State Christopher visited Beijing aiming at a full recovery of normal relations; the Taiwan issue was the central topic of the meeting (*New York Times,* Nov. 22, 1996: A8; Internet FBIS-CHI, Nov. 21, 1996). In the same month, President Clinton met President Jiang Zemin at Manila's Asia-Pacific Economic Cooperation (APEC) conference, and both agreed to exchange state visits next year (Internet New York Times, Nov. 25, 1996). In December, Chinese defense minister Chi Haotian visited the United States and started a comprehensive military dialogue on various issues ranging from Taiwan to nuclear non-proliferation (Internet Defense Link News, Dec. 9, 1996).

If Sino-U.S. relations had undergone episodes of crisis and damage-repair between 1989 and 1996, then the two governments attempted to walk out of the post-Tiananmen diplomacy to build a "strategic partnership" in 1997. The new foreign-policy initiative was coupled with the reshuffled Clinton administration and the 15th CCP Congress. However, the Taiwan issue remains the crux of the bilateral relationship, which is further complicated by respective domestic politics.

Sino-U.S. relations started in 1997 with the death of Deng Xiaoping in February. Just before the funeral for the paramount leader, Beijing indicated unambiguously to Secretary of State Madeleine Albright that China was eager to press ahead with improved U.S. ties. Albright said that she was "gratified by the warm reception" from President Jiang Zemin and other top Chinese leaders (*Wall Street Journal,* Feb. 25, 1997: 1, 24).

In March, Vice President Al Gore visited Beijing and signed two business deals worth almost US$2 billion: a purchase by the Chinese of five Boeing 777 jetliners for US$685 million and a US$1.3 billion joint venture by the General Motors Corporation and a state-owned Chinese enterprise to produce 100,000 Buick Century and Regal Sedans a year in Shanghai. Gore's decision to attend the signings was welcomed by American business groups and the Chinese leadership. Beijing wanted to demonstrate that, after Deng's death, new leaders can manage the all-important relationship with the United States. Further, China signed a third agreement to permit the United States to retain its consulate in Hong Kong after the British colony reverts to Chinese rule in June (Internet New York Times, Mar. 25, 1997).

In the same month, the Chinese navy made its port visit to the mainland United States, sailing into San Diego Bay just a year after U.S. aircraft carriers made a show of force in the Taiwan Strait. Wang Yongguo, commander of the visiting ship group from the South China Sea Fleet, said that the visit was of great historic significance and indicated a new stage in the exchange of the two navies (Internet FBIS-CHI, Mar. 26, 1997).

In May, top U.S. military officer General John Shalikashvili visited China and spoke at the PLA National Defense University. Shalikashvili said that Washington wanted more Sino-U.S. exchanges and a military maritime and air cooperation agreement that would cut the risk of miscalculations (Reuter in Early Bird, May 14, 1997). Since the end of 1996, Sino-U.S. military contacts have been mainly conducted in four respects: mutual high-level visits, exchanges and contacts between generals and field officers of the two armies, measures to increase mutual trust, and joint participation in forums on multilateral security (*Wen Wei Po,* May 8, 1997: A3).

As in the past several years, however, U.S.-China relations continued to be influenced by issues such as human rights and weapons proliferation. In early 1997, the U.S. government issued its annual human rights report which criticized China's retreat on human rights in 1996 (Internet New York Times, Jan. 28, 1997). In response, China reported the U.S. human rights problems in racial discrimination, the homeless, and other social and political respects (*China Daily,* Mar. 5, 1997: 4–5).

In May, the United States imposed sanctions against two Chinese companies, accusing them of knowingly helping Iran make chemical weapons (*New York Times,* May 23, 1997: 1). The U.S. State Department also informed Congress that China sold to Iran cruise missiles that challenged U.S. forces in the Persian Gulf. The State Department report confirmed that "China transferred a number of C-802 ship-based anti-ship cruise missiles to Iran" (*Washington Post,* May 31, 1997: 15). A CIA report called China and Russia the key suppliers of most destructive arms and technology in the latter half of 1996. China "provided a tremendous variety of assistance to both Iran's and Pakistan's ballistic missile programs" and "also was the primary source of nuclear related equipment and technology to Pakistan, and a key supplier to Iran" of such nuclear equipment (*Washington Post,* July 2, 1997: 24). China denied the CIA report.

Above all, however, the Taiwan issue remains volatile and potentially explosive. An article in *China Daily* urged the U.S. forces to leave East Asia (Mar. 19, 1997: 4). Meeting Vice President Gore in March, President Jiang said that the core of the three Sino-U.S. joint communiques is to establish the guiding principles for dealing with the Taiwan issue. He stressed that the Taiwan issue has, on many occasions, interfered with and even undermined the process of improving and developing Sino-U.S. relations (Internet FBIS-CHI, Mar. 28, 1997).

A few days after Gore left, House Speaker Gingrich visited China in March and warned a Chinese official that "we want you to understand, we will defend Taiwan. Period." Gingrich believed that China's top leaders were aware now that the United States would defend Taiwan if it were militarily attacked. Asked about Gingrich's statements, a Clinton administration official said that Gingrich "was speaking for himself" (Internet New York Times, Mar. 31, 1997).

The Sino-U.S. relationship, snared in the Taiwan issue, is further complicated by domestic politics. In 1997, the U.S. Congress launched a lengthy campaign investigating the Clinton administration's accused improper political fund-raising activities and sought a possible link between China's financial contributions to the Democratic National Committee before the 1996 presidential campaign and a favorable policy toward China (Internet Washington Post, Feb. 13, 1997). It was even reported that top Chinese leaders were linked to a plan to buy the U.S.

favor (*Washington Post,* Apr. 25, 1997: A1, A13). As a *New York Times* report said, "China is becoming a touchstone in domestic partisan politics in a way it has not seen since the early 1950s, when arguments raged over 'who lost China' to the Communists" (Internet, Apr. 29, 1997).

China denied all the allegations. Reportedly, FBI officials also believed that charges against China's money influence were overblown (*U.S. News & World Report,* July 21, 1997: 31). Referring to Gingrich's statements on Taiwan, a Chinese Foreign Ministry spokesman admonished the United States to speak with one voice on foreign policy and accused Gingrich of "improper statements." (Internet New York Times, Apr. 4, 1997). During White House national security advisor Samuel Berger's visit in Beijing, Liu Huaqiu, a Chinese State Council official, complained about what China's leaders perceived as widespread anti-China sentiment in Congress. In fall 1997, bills pending in Congress reflected bipartisan hostility toward China's human rights abuse and trade practices (*Washington Post,* Aug. 15, 1997: A28).

Fraught with all the above disputes, U.S.-China relations endured and even endeavored to make a breakthrough in 1997. In China, pro-U.S. officials and scholars began to envision the necessity to develop a "strategic partnership" with the United States. One article suggested that "if China and the United States want to establish a relationship of strategic partnership, figures of insight from the two sides should be concerned about the intention and extension of this 'partnership'" (*Wen Wei Po,* Aug. 11, 1997: A3). At a forum on Sino-U.S. relations in Shanghai, experts such as Ding Xinghao and Chen Peirao vigorously advocated a redefined Sino-U.S. strategic framework (*China Daily,* Sept. 4, 1997: 4).

As for China, a "partnership" stands for more than an ordinary "constructive relationship," and is second only to an "alliance." Beijing's top expectations of such a partnership are two: (1) getting the U.S. endorsement on China's WTO membership; and (2) coordinating with the United States to press Taiwan to follow the One Country Two Systems principle. China's new U.S. policy received support from many top military officers in Beijing (*Chung Yang Jih Pao,* Aug. 1, 1997: 2).

A partnership, of course, has to be an arrangement between Beijing and Washington. After Lee Teng-hui's visit to the United States in 1995 and the Taiwan crisis in March 1996, the United States adjusted its policy toward Taiwan. Washington was not pleased about Taiwan's aggressive attempts for independence or the UN status. Taiwan's intention to revise its constitution also caused Washington's concerns about instability across the Taiwan Strait. Instead, Assistant Secretary of State Stanley Roth told a press conference that Beijing's One Country Two Systems coincided with the U.S. status quo policy. Further, Secretary Albright implied that the United States would mediate the cross-Strait relationship, long desired by Beijing (*United Daily News,* Aug. 18, 1997: 3).

President Jiang Zemin's state visit to the United States in October 1997, the first in 12 years, was a landmark in Sino-U.S. relations. Jiang made his first stop at Pearl Harbor, a gesture to remind people of long-lasting Sino-U.S. common interests that stretch back to World War II, when they united against Japan. Despite their colorful debate on human rights in Washington, President Jiang and President Clinton achieved a series of accords at the summit:

- Hold regular strategic dialogues at every level of their governments;
- Establish a hotline to provide a direct communications link between the two presidents;
- Increase U.S. support of China's developing legal system, training lawyers, prosecutors, and judges;
- Step up anti-drug and anti-crime cooperation, allowing the United States to open a Drug Enforcement Administration office in Beijing;
- Accept a Military Maritime Consultative Agreement to handle incidents at sea by establishing closer communications and rules to handle encounters between the nations' ships and submarines;
- Sign a deal for the Chinese to buy 50 Boeing airplanes for US$3 billion; and
- Sign a pact allowing U.S. companies to sell civilian nuclear power reactors and technology in China worth US$60 billion; in turn, China pledges to end nuclear cooperation with Iran (*Washington Post,* Oct. 30, 1997: 15).

In January 1998, Defense Secretary William Cohen visited a secret underground air defense command and control center near Beijing, making the first tour of the site by a foreign delegation. Cohen and his Chinese counterpart, Chi Haotian, also signed the agreement aimed at avoiding clashes or accidents at sea between the naval forces of the two countries (*Washington Post,* Jan. 19, 1998: 19). In February, former top U.S. defense officials William Perry, John Shalikashivili, and Brent Scowcroft visited Taiwan and told its political leaders that "independence could be a catastrophe" and that as a result Taiwan should not count on U.S. military support (*Washington Post,* Feb. 21, 1998: 16).

In June 1998, President Clinton paid a historic visit to China. He accepted the welcome ceremony at Tiananmen Square and reviewed the PLA honor guard. His debate with President Jiang Zemin on human rights was broadcast live in China. In addition to all these profound political breakthroughs, the two countries signed a series of major agreements, including de-targeting their strategic nuclear missiles aimed at each other and tightening export controls on missile technology, equipment, materials, and expertise to South Asia, where India and Pakistan just conducted nuclear tests and started a nuclear arms race a month ago (White House Website, June 27, 1998). In Shanghai, President Clinton stated that the United States does not support an independent Taiwan, will oppose Taiwan's entry into organizations of sovereign states, and does not support a policy of "one China, one Taiwan."

SUMMARY

We have examined how the Taiwan issue has influenced the current Sino-U.S. relationship. Our study indicates that, as military balance continues its status quo across the Strait, China and the United States hold different perspectives on the Taiwan issue, respond to different domestic needs, and even precipitate hostile military actions. The differences are so profound and irreversible that their bilateral relations have suffered a series of downturns including those during 1995 and 1996. We cannot even exclude the possibility that mainland China would launch a military campaign against Taiwan; consequently, the Sino-U.S. relationship may fall in a direct military confrontation. Our systemic investigation of the impact of the Taiwan issue, however, also suggests a second possibility. Similarities between Chinese and American perceptions, relatively stable or peace-favoring domestic factors, as well as often restrained and cooperative behaviors by the two great powers may result in improved ties and greater regional stability and harmony.

Among all the factors we have addressed in this chapter, domestic situation—and economic development in particular—is perhaps the most important one in stabilizing the Sino-U.S. relationship. Despite some hostile rhetoric and increasing military power across the Taiwan Strait, neither the United States nor China believe that they should resort to a fight to resolve their disputes. Economic development and cooperation is their priority and it is in their common interest to avoid confrontation.

It must be noted that Japan is a crucial player in the Sino-U.S. relationship and in the development of the Taiwan situation. After winning a war over the Chinese at the end of the nineteenth century, Japan ruled Taiwan for about 50 years. Today, some Japanese and Taiwanese still want to see Taiwan as part of Japan. From 1997 to 1998, when the United States and Japan extended their alliance mission but refused to clarify its scope over Taiwan, China feared that the alliance would support Taiwan in case of a crisis. Chinese officials have warned many times against such a possibility. Other possible Japanese actions, such as participating in a missile defense system in East Asia led by the United States, building up strategic offensive power, and reversing non-nuclear policy, also worry China and will eventually affect Sino-U.S. relations.

Between Japan and the United States, China has urged both countries to follow the One China policy. The difference is that China encourages the United States to mediate the cross-Strait relationship, but asks Japan to refrain from intervening in the Taiwan question (*Ta Kung Pao,* Feb. 16, 1998).

Nevertheless, Japan is just as much concerned with economy as China and the United States, and would not readily sacrifice its relationship with China for the sake of Taiwan. In both political and military dimensions, Japan also has appeared to be less willing to exercise its influence than China and the United States, and therefore will have limited impact on their relationship.

NOTES

1. The Nine-Point Proposal contains the following proposals (see *Beijing Review,* Oct. 5, 1981: 10–11):

> (1) [T]alks be held between the Communist Party of China and the Kuomingtang of China on a reciprocal basis . . . ;
> (2) [T]he two sides make arrangements to facilitate the exchange of mails, trade, air and shipping services . . . ;
> (3) After the country is reunified, Taiwan can enjoy a high degree of autonomy as a special administrative region and it can retain its armed forces;
> (4) Taiwan's current socio-economic system will remain unchanged, so will its way of life and its economic and cultural relations with foreign countries;
> (5) People . . . in Taiwan may take up posts of leadership in national political bodies and participate in running the state;
> (6) When Taiwan's local finance is in difficulty, the Central Government may subsidize it as is fit for the circumstances;
> (7) For people . . . in Taiwan who wish to come and settle on the

mainland, it is guaranteed that proper arrangements will be made for them, . . . ;

(8) Industrialists and businessmen in Taiwan are welcome to invest and engage in various economic understandings on the mainland . . . ; and

(9) The reunification of the motherland is the responsibility of all Chinese.

2. As Deng himself explained, the One Country Two Systems concept had been in the making since 1978. But it seems that it was in 1984 that Chinese leaders and press started to use the term. As *Beijing Review* clearly defined it, " 'The one country, two systems' concept is that in the People's Republic of China, the one billion people on the mainland practices socialism while Hongkong and Taiwan remain capitalist" (Oct. 29, 1984: 16).

3. Although many people in the United States may tend not to even know the geographic location of Taiwan, public opinion holds that Taiwan and China are two countries and, therefore, Taiwan should enjoy everything as an independent state. The American public is an important factor in this regard.

4. The incentives of the U.S. arms sale to Taiwan deserve further analysis. As previously mentioned, one motive is to counter the capabilities of the mainland. In addition, it is obvious that U.S. sales help the American domestic economy, especially in an election year (the F-16 sale is a case in point). The U.S. share of the world weapons market today is as large as 70 percent. When the Pentagon's buying declines in the 1990s, the U.S. weapons manufacturers look to overseas markets. While the value of British, Chinese, and Russian arms exports declined dramatically (by more than 50 percent) in the 1990s, the value of U.S. contracts climbed 134 percent. Taiwan was the second largest buyer from the U.S. arsenal, consuming US$7.8 billion between 1990 and 1993 (*Time,* Dec. 12, 1994: 46–57). Thus, U.S. arms sales are not only military-strategic in nature, but also related to politics and economics.

3

U.S.-Japan Security Alliance: The Trial of a New Mission

The U.S.-Japan Security Treaty was originally signed in 1950 when Asia was divided between the Communist bloc and the non-Communist group. Forty years later, the Cold War came to its end and the U.S.-Japan security alliance faces a crossroads. What next? A new rationale for its existence and for its future mission envisioned in the 1997 Defense Cooperation Guidelines has finally opened another stage of the alliance development. This chapter probes the military alliance from the perspective of official perception, the domestic factor, and military power, and observes how these elements have influenced bilateral behavior within the military alliance.

CHANGING PERCEPTIONS

Japan

Japan is a minor military partner within the U.S.-Japan security alliance. Since the end of World War II, it has been under the umbrella of protection provided by the U.S. military presence in and around Japan. Whereas the United States provides power, Japan offers support. Nevertheless, Japan also has been an equal military partner in determining the necessity to keep the U.S. troops on its soil. Thus, Japan's attitude toward the bilateral security treaty is crucial for the continuity of the military alliance.

Japan's alliance policy is, first of all, based upon its assessment of Asia-Pacific security. In its 1997 Defense White Paper, Japan stated its belief that while the possibility of another world war is remote, the world is fraught with complex and diverse regional conflicts. Russia has scaled down but maintained massive armed forces in East Asia. Many countries are modernizing and expanding their military capabilities. Potential crises in the Korean Peninsula and other areas remain unsettled. The East Asian Strategic Review 1997–98, conducted by the National Institute for Defense Studies, states that Japan, the United States, China, and Russia are seeking a balance of power; as they are attempting to improve relations, the four major powers also work to hold the others in check. The report advises dialogues and confidence-building among all parties (Internet JDA).

Japan's official view of the security alliance is illustrated in *The Modality of the Security and Defense Capability of Japan: The Outlook for the 21st Century* (hereafter, *Modality*), a report provided by the Advisory Group on Defense Issues in 1994. (The advisory group was chaired by Hirotaro Higuchi and joined by members from corporations and universities). Japan's view is composed of at least three main factors. First, the United States retains military supremacy in the post–Cold War era. Nevertheless, "the United States no longer holds an overwhelming advantage in terms of overall national strength. . . . Consequently, there is a possibility that competitive relations will intensify over economic issues" between the United States and other countries (Advisory Group 1994: 2–3).

Second, in the post–Cold War international security system, multilateral cooperation is crucial and the question is whether the United States "will be able to demonstrate leadership in multilateral cooperation." "The mechanism of resolving security problems through international cooperation is still imperfect, but it is showing signs of developing little by little, both on the level of the United Nations and on the regional level" (Advisory Group 1994: 3).

Finally, "in order to further ensure the security of Japan and make multilateral security cooperation effective, close and broad cooperation and joint work between Japan and the United States are essential. The institutional framework for this is provided by the Japan-U.S. Security Treaty" (Advisory Group 1994: 10).

No matter how implicit these points are, Japan's attitude shows burgeoning changes within the U.S.-Japan alliance; in other words, Japan desires to take a multilateral approach toward international security issues. Meanwhile, and perhaps relatedly, Japan wishes to see the U.S.-Japan alliance go beyond defending Japan to cover a larger portion of the Asia-Pacific region:

> The Japan-U.S. Security Treaty remains an indispensable precondition for the defense of Japan even in the post–Cold War security environment. What is more, the range of fields in which Japan and the United States can cooperate for the security of Asia is expected to widen. In other words, the Japan-U.S. relationship of cooperation in the area of security must be considered not only from the bilateral viewpoint but, at the same time, also from the broader perspective of security in the entire Asia/Pacific region (Advisory Group 1994: 16).

The endorsement of a continued U.S.-Japan alliance and the inclination for both a multilateral approach and a more active Japanese role—a new mission in the post Cold War era—is fostered by not only official but also non-official opinions. If we categorize government officials and their supporters as "mainstream," there are at least two other influential groups: nationalists and pacifists (see Fukuyama and Oh 1993; Tamamoto 1992; Sasae 1994: 15). Of course, the three groups overlap with each other.

Mainstreamers include officials in the Ministry of Foreign Affairs (MOFA), the Japan Defense Agency (JDA), the Self-Defense Forces (SDF), the Liberal Democratic Party (LDP), and conservative think tanks. The LDP's "Party Campaign Platform for 1995," for example, made the following statement:

> Even after the end of the Cold War, Japan-U.S. relations are the most important bilateral relationship in creating peace and prosperity in the world, especially in the Asia-Pacific region. Therefore, we will continue to firmly maintain the Japan-U.S. security system (FBIS-EAS, Aug. 1, 1996: 16).

Within the mainstream, there are at least two kinds of advocates for new directions of the bilateral alliance. On the one side are political-commercial realists who tend to downplay the significance of Japan's independent military readiness and rather favor an economic contribution to the maintenance of the security treaty. They strongly support Japanese burden-sharing to keep U.S. forces in Japan because they benefit Japan's political and economic interests. Important proponents of political-commercial realism include former finance minister and prime minister Kiichi Miyazawa. But they are beginning to understand that Japan needs to do more than just write paychecks to support the bilateral alliance (Fukuyama and Oh 1993: 26; Tamamoto 1992, 228–229). Hitoshi Tanaka, councilor of the MOFA's North American Affairs Bureau, wrote that Japan "cannot but be involved directly" in the Asia-Pacific security issues. "The final destination" for the U.S.-Japan security alliance is "more bilateral and more reliable" (Internet FBIS-EAS, Nov. 21, 1996).

On the other side are military realists or defense specialists who believe that economic cooperation aside, Japan must bear greater political and military responsibility to the bilateral security treaty. They argue that the SDF needs to upgrade its command, control, communications, and intelligence (C^3I), and to establish an independent military power. In the meantime, Japan and the United States must create a forum for security dialogue and increase mutual understanding and the effectiveness of the alliance (Fukuyama and Oh 1993: 27; Tamamoto 1992: 229). In the mid 1990s, military realism has tended to dominate mainstream thinking. Japan's "National Defense Program Outline in and after FY 1996" (NDPO) expounds:

> While the principal mission of the Self-Defense Forces continues to be the defense of Japan, the Self-Defense Forces . . . will also have to be prepared for various situations such as large-scale disasters . . . , and play an appropriate role in a timely manner in the government's active efforts to establish a more stable security environment.

The NDPO also lays out the contents of Japan's defense capability and concludes that "Japan's defense structure must possess adequate flexibility so that smooth response can be made to changing situations" (Internet, Japan's MOFA, Dec. 1995).

Mainstream military realists include political strongmen such as former prime minister Yasuhiro Nakasone. They are not satisfied with Japan's current international status and vigorously pursue a full great power status. Prominent political leaders, such as the New Frontier Party leader Ichiro Ozawa and the LDP's Ryutaro Hashimoto, all wrote books advocating a Japan that is independent and stands on its own feet, although they also acknowledged the significance of a U.S.-Japan alliance (Ozawa 1994; Hashimoto 1994). In this regard, military realists are somewhat linked with "nationalists."

Nationalists are not affiliated with any significant government institution or political party, but are individuals found in all corners of Japanese society. Nationalists contend that Japan must prepare to defend itself and be independent from U.S. protection. The first step toward a great power Japan, they propose, is to revise the constitution that prohibits a strong Japanese military machine and denounces war as a means against other nations (Sato 1996). In reality, since the end of World War II, Japan has quietly expanded its military operations. "Military" is no longer a dirty word, and the SDF has become respectable again. Although a career in the forces remains a reluctant choice, young people are no longer automatically anti-SDF as they were before (*Far Eastern Economic Review,* Sept. 19, 1996: 16–17).

A leading nationalist is perhaps Shintaro Ishihara, a LDP member and the co-author of *The Japan That Can Say No.* Ishihara resents that Japan has blindly followed America's lead in foreign policy since the end of World War II. He claims that it is time for Japan to form an autonomous foreign and security policy without the U.S. dominance. "Today, the security treaty is no longer indispensable" (Ishihara 1991: 50, 55–56). Another prominent nationalist, Jun Eto, contends that the United States is often flawed in its demands on Japan and in its illusion as a leader of a new world order. He argues for a revised Japanese constitution to permit the dispatch of Japanese forces overseas (Eto 1991).

Pacifists mostly come from the academic community and the Socialist Democratic Party (SDP). Pacifist proposals traditionally urged Japan to contribute to the collective United Nations leadership and terminate its security treaty with the United States. As an opposition force, the SDP had advocated that Japan maintain a peace constitution and reduce Japan's military capabilities. A professor at Tokyo's Meiji Gakuin University argued that "the U.S.-Japan Security Treaty is an anti-Soviet treaty and this justification for it has collapsed. . . . The American policy of bilateral treaties hardens antagonisms in Asia and stops real peace in the region" (*Far Eastern Economic Review,* Nov. 23, 1995: 20, 22). Government officials often ignored the SDP and scholars' demands, and pacifists did not become "official" until decades after World War II.

Prime Minister Tomiichi Murayama of the SDP made two unprecedented changes during 1994 and 1995. First, after the LDP stayed in power for more than three decades but lost its dominance of the government in August 1993, the LDP and SDP formed a coalition government in 1994 led by an SDP prime minister. For the first time since 1948, the SDP became a ruling party. Second, despite its traditional ideology, the SDP turned to support the U.S.-Japan Security Treaty and, therefore, continued the LDP's mainstream policy (Satoh 1995: 279). The SDP-LDP coalition might only appear expedient, but illustrates the differences and overlap of various schools of thought in Japan. The SDP's "Manifesto for the Year 1995" stated that "while firmly maintaining the Japan-U.S. Security Treaty, we will try to reduce the treaty's military-related aspects and to expand its political and economic aspects. . . ." (FBIS-EAS, Aug. 1, 1996: 17).

In sum, there are at least three changing components comprising the Japanese perception of the U.S.-Japan alliance. First, it is to Japan's fundamental national interest to maintain the bilateral alliance. Second, the alliance aside, Japan wishes to take a broader and multilateral approach toward international security issues. Finally, Japan hopes to increase its military power and elevate its status within the alliance. At present, the U.S.-Japan alliance remains viable and appears to be able to continue for a long time. Nevertheless, as Japanese opinions tend to favor a multilateral security mechanism and start to consider a more independent military force, the U.S.-Japan alliance will inevitably enter a period of adjustment or even decline. After years of debate on a new Japanese role in the international system, Japan seems to have achieved a broader consensus on a more multilateral and more independent mission, despite the continued favor of a U.S.-Japan alliance (see *Opinion Analysis,* Sept. 11, 1996: 1; Nishi 1996: 49).

In a broader context, it is worth noting the China factor related to the U.S.-Japan alliance. Japan's assessment of China directly affects the goal of the U.S.-Japan alliance in the 1990s. Former prime minister Miyazawa stated that "the current Chinese leaders all say they want peace, and I believe they are being honest. But in 15 years, when it is more powerful, Japan and the U.S. will need to form a dialogue with China—a 'trialogue'—and the Japan-U.S. relationship will be the linchpin of this. This is the new role for the Japan-U.S. security treaty" (*Far Eastern Economic Review,* Nov. 23, 1995: 20). Despite the increasing worry of Chinese military buildup in the 1990s, it seems that many Japanese officials are holding such a cautious and hopeful view of China with respect to the U.S.-Japan alliance (see chapter 4).

United States

In the early 1990s, the Bush administration outlined an assessment of East Asia security and a process for restructuring and reducing U.S. forces in the region. Two Pentagon reports (East Asian Strategic Initiative—EASI) scheduled three stages of U.S. troop reduction in East Asia: phase one, 1990 to 1992; phase two, 1993–1995; phase three, 1995 to 2000 (U.S. Department of Defense 1990; 1992). The Bush administration in its last few months and then the Clinton administration, however, ended the EASI reduction of the U.S. presence in East Asia. The Clinton administration's East Asian Strategic Review (EASR) instead declared the U.S. commitment to maintain a forward deployment of about 100,000 troops in the region (about 47,000 in Japan). The reason is, as Defense Secretary Cohen reiterated, that Asia remains a concentration of powerful states with sizable militaries, some nuclear-armed; a region of great global economic importance; and an area with numerous navigational choke points (Cohen 1998). As far as Japan is concerned,

> There is no more important bilateral relationship than the one we have with Japan. It is fundamental to both our Pacific security policy and our global strategic objectives. Our security alliance with Japan is the linchpin of United States security policy in Asia.

This paragraph from the 1995 *United States Security Strategy for the East Asia-Pacific Region* (U.S. Department of Defense Office of International Security Affairs, Feb. 1995: 10) highlights the current U.S. official attitude toward the U.S.-Japan security treaty and its future. Defense Secretary William Perry reiterated a year later that "the security and the stability of this region depend on the continued friendship and the continued alliance between the United States and Japan" (Perry 1996: 2).

Responding to some proposed security alternatives, Assistant Secretary of Defense Joseph Nye discredited the rationale to replace U.S. bilateral alliances with loose regional institutions. Instead, he argued, "reinforcing our alliances to identify their new basis after the Cold War is at the heart of" the U.S. security strategy (Nye 1995: 94–95).

It seems that there has been a consensus at the top level of the Clinton administration about the revitalization of a U.S.-Japan security alliance. This belief is also shared by many specialists and scholars. One analyst wrote that the U.S.-Japan Security Treaty

> provides a framework defining the fundamental bilateral ties of the two countries. In this sense, the drafters of the treaty may have understood something better than many people today: that "threats" may come and go but values are enduring.

> What has been crucial for U.S.-Japan security cooperation has not
> been that Japanese and U.S. threat perceptions are identical, but that
> they are sufficiently overlapping to undergird a sense of broad com-
> mon interests (Levin 1993: 73).

Washington, however, is not certain about how far and at what speed Japan should become a great power that can contribute to U.S. operations in East Asia or any crisis in the world. Notwithstanding the logic of enlarging deterrence and agility of the U.S.-Japan alliance, another logic of restraining Japanese expansion and not intensifying regional geopolitical frictions because of the rise of Japanese militarism also applies that it would be imprudent to push Japan too far and too quickly (Mochizuki 1997: 19–20). Washington understands that a new Japanese capability is a sensitive issue in East Asia.

Many Japan-watchers in the United States have otherwise noted that future bilateral defense relations will embark on a much rockier road. Douglas Stuart and William Tow have suggested that the rising multipolar regional order in East Asia will be less open to U.S. interests and influence than the web of a bilateral defense system. The rationale for the San Francisco system (a series of bilateral military alliances signed in San Francisco in the early 1950s) no longer exists in a world where the Soviet Union has collapsed and Asia has become a world economic power center (1995: 6). Kenneth Pyle poses that "the new conditions in Asia suggest that the U.S. approach to Asia-Pacific security should be rethought, with greater emphasis on multilateral arrangements, mutuality, consensus, and local contribution" (1992: 143).

The American reading of Japan's new defense strategy similarly highlights limitations exposed from the alliance. American analysts believed that the *Modality*'s attention to the bilateral defense relationship is "overshadowed" by Japan's focus on multilateralism and autonomous capabilities. "As it now stands, the report's recommendations suggest that multilateralism is a hedge against waning U.S. commitments to the alliance, and possibly even a distraction (in terms of political and financial resources) from bilateral defense cooperation" (Cronin and Green 1994: 9). In this regard, many in the United States have viewed an expanded Japanese share of defense responsibility with the United States as a necessary step to sustain the security alliance (Manning 1995: 96; Pyle 1996). These concerns, therefore, have raised a question about the feasibility of the U.S.-Japan alliance under new conditions in the 1990s and beyond. The alliance will likely face unabated challenges to its obligations, functions, and scopes in the coming century.

Despite various concerns and even suspicions, political leaders in both countries are determined about the value of the U.S.-Japan Security Treaty. In April 1996, President Clinton visited Tokyo and the message from him and Prime Minister Hashimoto confirmed their commitment:

- Japan and the United States approach the 21st century as allies and partners with shared values, interests and hopes. Our relationship is of bilateral, regional and global importance. We face the challenges of tomorrow strengthened by years of common tests, experiences and cooperation.
- Our alliance is central to peace, stability and prosperity in the Asia-Pacific region. Japan-U.S. security arrangements are vital to both nations.
- We have promoted cooperation and a sense of community among the countries in the Asia-Pacific region (FBIS-EAS, Apr. 18, 1996: 1–2).

Entering 1996, the U.S.-Japan alliance seemed to be motivated by a new concern—China, and especially its military exercises over Taiwan in March. Officially, United States and Japan have not declared China as a threat. According to an official Japanese news release, Prime Minister Hashimoto "considered the positive engagement of China in the international community to be important." During the summit, President Clinton also endorsed the One China policy. The two leaders urged a peaceful resolution of the Taiwan question (FBIS-EAS, Apr. 18, 1996: 8).

Numerous news reports suspect that the China threat has provided a new dynamic for the U.S.-Japan security alliance toward the twenty-first century. Many analysts in both Japan and the United States believe that the alliance has a new target that is China (FBIS-EAS, Apr. 18, 1996: 18; *U.S. News & World Report*, Apr. 22, 1996: 49; *New York Times,* Apr. 21, 1996: Section IV-5). Yet, an overall examination would not support such a speculation (see chap 5). Even when Washington and Tokyo started to revise the 1978 U.S.-Japan Defense Cooperation Guidelines in late 1996, Defense Secretary William Perry pointed out that the goal would also benefit China and other nations in the region (U.S. Department of State Dispatch, Sept. 23, 1996: 473). The U.S. government has at least played down the possibility of using the alliance against China.

In any event, under all kinds of anxiety, the text of U.S.-Japan Defense Cooperation Guidelines was released in New York on September 23, 1997. The gist of the guidelines includes: basic premises and principles, cooperation under normal circumstances, actions in response to an armed attack against Japan, cooperation in areas surrounding Japan, and bilateral programs for effective defense cooperation (Internet FBIS-EAS, Sept. 24, 1997). The core of the guidelines is bilateral actions in response to armed attack against Japan at various stages. The guidelines stipulate that Japan will take primary responsibility to repel such attack whereas the United States will provide appropriate support to Japan. The most controversial part of the guidelines is the concept of "areas surrounding Japan." It is not only related to Japan's constitution in terms of the use of armed forces but also concerns the international community, principally China and the two Koreas. Aware of the dilemma, the guidelines only offer an ambiguous answer: "The concept, situations in areas surrounding Japan, is not geographic but situational."

In sum, official policies in both Washington and Tokyo wish to maintain and even somewhat expand the mission of the U.S.-Japan alliance. This official view also is broadly shared by experts in both countries. The difference, however, lies in the U.S. pursuit of a stronger alliance with greater Japanese contribution and Japan's increasing interest in a more multilateral and independent military strategy. Under a grand consensus, the bilateral alliance is compounded with diversified motivations, expectations, and even suspicions.

DOMESTIC CONSTRAINTS

Japan

At the end of the World War II in 1945, the U.S. troops occupied Japan. In five years, Japan underwent unprecedented economic, political, and military reform imposed by the U.S. military authority. Since 1950, Japan has embarked on a road of autonomy, but has always been a U.S. ally, a policy known as the Yoshida Doctrine. Thus, the U.S.-Japan alliance has been naturally part of Japanese domestic life, which, in turn, exerts complex influence on the bilateral alliance.

Nowadays, many in Japan have called for expanding the SDF and revising Article 9 of the constitution to exercise the right to collective self-defense (Sato 1992: 185–186). While a more assertive SDF may contribute to a stronger U.S.-Japan alliance, geographic location, racial identity as an Asian nation, and the hierarchical social structure constitute other important characteristics shaping Japan's foreign behavior (Unger 1993: 13). These factors affect Japan's "national personalities" (Tamamoto 1993: 38). In the following pages, we focus on Japan's political-government structure, domestic economic concerns, political identity, and public opinion, and their impact on the implementation of foreign policy.

In 1994, Japan reelected three prime ministers, and the political vulnerability of the government caused doubts about its actual authority. Japan's leadership, in this sense, may have entered a period of disarray. The weakness of the Japanese prime ministers, in turn, posed a challenge to any effective Japanese international leadership.

MOFA, the Ministry of Finance (MOF), the Ministry of International Trade and Industry (MITI), and the JDA are the major institutions with respect to Japan's national security. The prime minister has little power over these ministries and his capability of decision making is consequently reduced. For instance, the prime minister exercises little control over the various offices in the Cabinet Secretariat, which is designated to coordinate relations between ministries. Except ministers and the parliamentary vice minister, the prime minister is not entitled to fill in political appointees in any major ministry. Instead, the prime minister's inner circle is staffed with people from the major ministries. Further, the prime minister is under pressure from various party factions and often accepts candidates recommended by each faction according to their experience in the Diet. This was highlighted by Prime Minister Ryutaro Hashimoto's difficulty in reshuffling his third cabinet in August-September 1997 (Internet FBIS-EAS, Sept. 12, 1997). He even apologized in his Diet policy speech about his "inability" and promised to "build a system where the prime minister can exercise stronger leadership, where the cabinet can act promptly . . . , and where all ministries and agencies can implement policies efficiently" (Internet FBIS-EAS, Sept. 30, 1997).

The JDA is embedded in the inter-ministerial coordination process and has little institutional autonomy. No security policy is made directly by the JDA; rather, MOF, MITI, and MOFA all have their own officials inside the JDA. The SDF officers within the JDA are subordinate to a layer of civilian personnel. As a result, military operations are under the diversified control of the civilian administration (Katzenstein and Okawara 1993a: 92–95; Unger 1993: 15). Each ministry has its own interests and priorities and, as a result, the inter-ministerial relations are characterized by "autarky:"

> The Ministry of Foreign Affairs aims to please the United States by increasing defense spending . . . ; the JDA appears more concerned with building its prestige and gaining more voice in defense policy than with constructing a respectable fighting force. Although the MOF claims that defense spending weakens Japan by diverting capital away

> from more productive industries, MITI argues that increased spending
> on defence strengthens industry. . . . (Zeringue and Kritenbrink 1994:
> 130).

The administrative structure, coinciding with Japanese national economic interests, assures political and economic concerns remain the priority in Japan's national security decision making. Even if the Japanese people grant the SDF greater authority and power, it will take many years for Japan to emerge as an effective military power in international society. After all, Japan needs a strong leader for both domestic and foreign affairs. This implies that Japan cannot soon become a normal or decisive military partner as the United States has insisted.

To understand the economic priority, it is important to note that Japan seeks economic gains through the implementation of its defense policies. The "economy first" principle has been accepted by major defense-related agencies. MITI supported the industry's objective of developing arms sales and stimulated critical industrial sectors such as the aircraft production. JDA aims to build a credible military by procuring sophisticated weapons through domestic industry. MOF simply opposes defense expenditure increases which it views as a drag on economic growth. Industry, in the meantime, pushes the "economy first" line in a persistent way; it finds that defense projects have not only opened overseas markets but also absorbed advanced technologies from the United States. The close relationship between the government and industry serves as a convenient channel for industry to influence, though not decisively, the course of defense policies in Tokyo (Chinworth 1992: xii–xiv).

The "economy first" factor has prevented Japan from becoming an active military power. That highlights different concerns by the United States and Japan and raises questions about the reliability of the military alliance during a crisis or wartime. The economic priority, however, does not necessarily distance Japan from the United States. Rather, Japan has and will continue to depend on U.S. support just because of its economic concerns. Japan needs consistent input of U.S. technology, bilateral cooperation on defense projects, and U.S. markets. In addition, security uncertainty in the Asia-Pacific region will only ensure Japan's adherence to the alliance with the United States until Japan feels confident enough to defend itself.

Government structure and economics aside, another domestic question is Japan's national and political identity that sheds light on the U.S.-Japan alliance. In theory, Japanese democracy converges with the United States in terms of political ideology; in turn, the two countries trust each other and sustain a high level of military cooperation. But in the 1970s and 1980s, Japan tried to advocate Japanese or Asian ways of security; the common sense of security seemed to be questionable.

At the same time, many Japanese observers believed that Japan's economic miracle occurred as a result of the unique features of Japanese capitalism, not of the adoption of European or American economic practices. They attributed Japan's success to indigenous traditional culture (Sato, Kumon, and Murakami 1976: 84–85; Iwata 1979). One author argued that the economic power of the United States had declined; on the verge of the collapse of the U.S.-dominated international economic order, it "is the time for Japan to begin speaking out and taking action to build a new order for the twenty-first century" (Kenjiro 1985: 14).

In the late 1990s, Japan is bogged down by its ailing economy; few Japanese are talking about Japan's leadership in the twenty-first century. Still, Tokyo warns the United States not to interfere in Japanese internal affairs by pushing Japan toward a large-scale economic restructuring (FBIS-EAS, Apr. 10, 1998). Nonetheless, the strong economic interdependence between the two countries cautioned the leaderships to stay away from any economic or political standoff. Shortly after Japan officially confirmed its economic recession in June 1998, the first one in 23 years, the U.S. government joined Tokyo in a dramatic rescue operation for the falling Japanese yen (*Washington Post,* June 13, 1998: 1; June 18, 1998: 1).

Addressing Japan's domestic situation, we cannot overlook the current public debate on the Japanese military role in international affairs. Since the end of the World War II, the Japanese public opinion has greatly influenced Tokyo's security policy. In the 1950s, the public debated on the constitutionality of the SDF and a revised U.S.-Japan Security Treaty; in the late 1960s and early 1970s, on the size and speed of Japan's military build-up; in the late 1970s and early 1980s, on the viability of Japan's greater defense capability; and in the 1990s, on the new mission of the SDF and the revision of the constitution (Sasae 1994: 15).

Nowadays, the Japanese public are generally cautious over an active military stance, overwhelmingly support Article 9 of the constitution, and lack willingness to resort to armed defense in international conflicts (Bobrow 1989: 597; *New York Times,* Sept. 9, 1996: A3). Japan's constitution renounces war as an instrument of national security policy. Article 9 imposes severe restraints on the Japanese military role and its development. Although they have gradually come to accept the necessity of the SDF and a reasonable national defense capability, the Japanese public have adamantly refused to amend Article 9 in a substantial way. "The normative constraints have made it impossible to revise Article 9 of the Constitution; to build nuclear weapons or to agree to their deployment on Japanese soil; to dispatch Japanese troops abroad in combatant roles . . . or to raise the JDA to ministerial status" (Katzenstein and Okawara 1993a: 104–105).

Japan did dispatch its troops to join the UN Peacekeeping Operations (UNPKO) in Cambodia in 1992. The significance lies in the fact that Japan, for the first time since 1945, sent military forces overseas, although the mission was restrictively underwritten by the UN. Under this framework, Japan later participated in UNPKOs in the Middle East and Africa. In April 1996, the United States and Japan signed the U.S.-Japan Joint Declaration on Security, by which Tokyo agreed to supply spare parts and services to the U.S. military when taking part in joint training and peacekeeping missions. All that might imply that both the Japanese public opinion and the government are tending to favor a larger military role abroad.

Nevertheless, such a public sympathy does not automatically extend into a stronger support of the U.S.-Japan alliance. The renewal of the U.S. bases in Japan has turned out to be a big thorn for Japanese public opinion, especially in the case of Okinawa, which hosts over 28,000 U.S. soldiers or 62 percent of the U.S. troops in Japan (*Far Eastern Economic Review,* Nov. 23, 1995: 20). In September 1995, three U.S. servicemen raped a 12–year-old school girl in Okinawa. For many Japanese who are resentful about five decades of U.S. military presence, the crime was the last insult. The rape incident unleashed a new wave of bitterness. A *Nihon Keizai Shimbun* poll showed opposition to the security treaty at 29 percent in August, but up to 40 percent in mid-October, while the percentage in favor of the treaty fell to 44 percent from 60 percent (*Far Eastern Economic Review,* Nov. 23, 1995: 16–17).

In late March 1996, Prime Minister Hashimoto endorsed the renewed lease of Okinawa island to the U.S. troops, but tensions between the public and the Japanese government/the U.S. troops remained. A poll conducted by *Asahi Shimbun* in May 1997 indicates that 72 percent of the responses favored a gradual reduction of the U.S. bases and 15 percent desired a total withdrawal. Further, 53 percent opposed the transfer of the Okinawan facilities to the main islands, while 38 percent supported such a move (*Asahi Shimbun,* May 12, 1997: 1, 10).

In the past, it was left-wing and extreme right-wing forces who called for the termination of the security treaty. In the 1990s, however, the voices also came from nationalists in the once center-right political spectrum (Inoguchi, 1995: 393). This trend is coupled with Japanese peripheral interest in defense issues—just over half of the Japanese in their 20s would fight to defend their country, reported in a *Yomiuri* survey (Blaker 1996: 49).

How do we assess the domestic factors as a whole? Japan's government bureaucracy, the mentality of "economy first," and public opinion will continue to set a brake on its military growth and the functioning of the U.S.-Japan alliance. As former Japanese prime minister Morihiro Hosokawa argued, "it is natural for the Japanese people to be skeptical of the U.S. military presence" in Japan, which "should fade with this century's end" (Hosokawa 1998: 5).

It is still years until Japan reaches a genuine social and political consensus. The Japanese priority is the pursuit of civilian economic-technological power. Despite current suspicion of the threat of China and security uncertainty in Asia, Japan's political structure and public opinion may postpone any rapid emergence of a "normal" military power. As a result, the U.S.-Japan alliance will continue to exist but can only evolve slowly.

United States

In this section, we analyze American domestic influence on the U.S.-Japan security alliance and discuss U.S. national interests, government structure, public opinion, and economic development. The discussion will show that American domestic factors are diversified and not decisively favorable to a continued U.S.-Japan security treaty and its designated commitments.

Official definitions of U.S. national interests by both George Bush and Bill Clinton's administrations embrace the survival of the nation, a healthy and growing economy, and vigorous relations with allies and friendly nations, as well as democracy and human rights. Analysts point out that national interests need to be clarified into categories of descending importance: national survival, vital interests, major interests, peripheral interests, and insubstantial interests. The relative importance of the various interests should determine the extent to which the United States employs military force on their behalf. The security alliance with Japan falls in the second category of vital interests, which mandate the use of any military means (Kugler 1994: 59–62; Sarkesian 1995: 7–8, 208–209).

It is interesting to note that the U.S. international security network is built on a mostly multilateral basis, which is composed of the Inter-American Treaty of Reciprocal Assistance (Rio Treaty), the North Atlantic Treaty Organization (NATO), and other multilateral defense arrangements such as the Australia, New Zealand, and United States

Treaty (ANZUS) (in 1986, the United States suspended security obligations to New Zealand). The United States is maintaining only three bilateral alliances—with Japan, South Korea, and the Philippines (Sarkesian
1995: 204) and has a security arrangement with Thailand. The U.S.-Japan
security alliance has been reiterated by the U.S. government as the sound-
est alliance in the world.

Similar to the complexity of Japan's government structure, however,
the U.S. policy instrument may not respond accurately to "vital interests"
concerning Japan. There are at least three major power clusters: (1) the
"policy triad," consisting of secretary of state, secretary of defense, and
national security advisor to the president; (2) the director of the CIA and
chairman of the joint chiefs of staff; and (3) the White House chief of
staff and counselor to the president. Or, divided in functions, they are (1)
president and his staff; (2) the military establishment; and (3) the intelligence establishment (Sarkesian 1995: 11–12). On the daily work, however, "coherence and reasonably effective functioning of the national
security system is not self-executing." Rather, the post–Cold War U.S.
security approach appears to be "a muddled policy process" (Sarkesian
1995: 243).

The most obvious disagreement often occurs between the defense
establishment and the Office of the United States Trade Representative
(USTR), and between the administration and Congress. The priorities of
the USTR are to assure open access to foreign markets for U.S. goods and
investment, negotiate trade treaties, and investigate foreign market barriers under Section 301 of the 1974 Trade Act. Economic goals have encountered security arrangements within the U.S.-Japan security alliance.
Suffering a long-term trade deficit trend from Japan, U.S. economic representatives question the rationale of U.S. protection of Japan and ask for
a larger burden to be shared by Japan.

Congress maintains a high profile on trade issues and puts the
administration under pressure to toughen demands on Tokyo. Two congressional committees take the lead: the Senate Committee on Finance
and the House Committee on Ways and Means. Weakened by frequent
turnover of the staff and senior politicians, U.S. agencies are often inter-
rupted and inconsistent in dealing with Japan on both economic and security issues (Donnelly 1993: 338–340).

A fundamental problem is related to Japan's role and the signifi-
cance of the U.S.-Japan alliance measured by U.S. national interests.
Assistant Defense Secretary Joseph Nye warned in 1995 that the United
States was dangerously taking the alliance for granted and criticized those

who complained about the deployment of the 100,000 U.S. troops in East Asia (*Economist,* May 13, 1995: 35). Opponents argue that the United States should keep the troops and the money at home. They suggest that with the end of the Cold War and the rise of Japanese economic power, there is no reason for the U.S. forces to protect an economic superpower like Japan (Bandow 1994; Johnson and Keehn 1995).

American public opinion has an unpredictable role and complicates the future of the U.S.-Japan military alliance. An early 1995 Gallup Organization survey showed that while three-quarters of intellectuals have a generally favorable view of Japan, only 34 percent of ordinary Americans do, with 46 percent of ordinary Americans having no opinion (SAIS 1996: 6). The Foreign Policy Leadership Project (FPLP) conducts nationwide surveys of American opinion leaders every four years. Based on the survey data, Ole Holsti and James Rosenau have provided findings on domestic opinion groups and their foreign policy preferences. The findings shed light on the possible impact of the public opinion on the sustainability of the U.S.-Japan alliance.

As indicated in the table, opinion leaders differ from official government attitudes toward the use of military force and military allies. The former are much more conservative and tend to rely on non-military means in international conflicts. They also are less willing to support U.S. allies. In another survey, only 28 percent think it is very important to protect weaker nations against foreign aggression and 34 percent are for defending allies' security (Holsti and Rosenau 1996: 46).

Some may argue that American public support of the security alliance with Japan remains strong. A February-March 1996 Gallup poll of both ordinary citizens and opinion leaders demonstrated that 66 percent of respondents believed that the U.S.-Japan alliance was in the U.S. national interest and 75 percent favored maintaining it. A May 1997 Louis Harris survey yielded a similar result: 79 percent supported the military alliance. But support of the alliance is still different from actual fight for Japan. This difference was reflected in the same Harris survey: 44 percent supported a gradual reduction of U.S. troops in Japan and 5 percent a total withdrawal. In the Gallup poll, 42 percent ordinary citizens and 66 percent of the opinion leaders wanted Japan to increase its capabilities for its own defense (Mochizuki 1997: 29).

If public opinion plays only a potential and indirect role in influencing the U.S.-Japan security alliance, U.S. domestic economics has displayed a much more powerful impact over time, and especially during the 1980s and the 1990s.

TABLE 3.1

Future Threats to American National Security, 1992 [FPLP]

To evaluate the seriousness of the following issues to American national security during the remaining years of this century	Percentage of respondents who evaluate threats as extremely serious [N=2,312]
A. The possession of nuclear weapons by Third World countries	62
B. An inability to solve such domestic problems as the decay of cities, homelessness, unemployment, racial conflict, and crime	60
C. The federal budget deficit*	54
D. International drug trafficking	41
E. Environmental problems, such as air pollution and water contamination	40
F. Uncontrolled growth of the world's population	37
G. A growing gap between rich and poor nations	27
H. The greenhouse effect	27
I. Nuclear weapons in former Soviet republics	25
J. Armed conflicts in the Middle East	16
K. American interventions in conflicts that are none of our business	13
L. Mass migrations	10

Source: Ole R. Holsti and James N. Rosenau, "Liberals, Populists, Libertarians, and Conservatives: The Link between Domestic and International Affairs," International Political Science Review, 17, No. 1 (1996): 42

*The federal budget deficit has changed to be surplus since 1997.

It seems that opinion leaders do not rank international security issues as serious threats to the United States, except nuclear weapons proliferation in the Third World countries. Rather, opinion leaders are much more concerned with domestic development and international non-military issues. This survey raises a question about how determined the United States would be in defending Japan if the latter faced a nuclear threat (Layne 1996: 72).

TABLE 3.2

U.S. International Roles and Interests, 1992 [FPLP]

Please indicate how strongly you agree or disagree with each statement	Percentage of respondents who agree strongly and agree somewhat [N=2,312]
A. U.S. foreign policy should supplement military preparedness with an equal focus on international economic and social issues	92
B. The United States should be as ready to form economic and diplomatic coalitions to cope with the world's problems of hunger and poverty as it is to lead military coalitions against aggressors	92
C. The United States should take all steps including the use of force to prevent aggression by any expansionist power	70
D. Our allies are perfectly capable of defending themselves and they can afford it, thus allowing the United States to focus on internal rather than external threats to its well-being	59
E. America's conception of its leadership role in the world must be scaled down	57
F. Vital interests of the United States are largely confined to Western Europe, Japan, and the Americas	29

Source: Ole R. Holsti and James N. Rosenau, "Liberals, Populists, Libertarians, and Conservatives: The Link between Domestic and International Affairs," International Political Science Review 17, No. 1 (1996): 44–45.

A group of U.S. government officials state:

> Although there are no signs that U.S.-Japan relations will turn hostile, Japan's rise as a global economic and financial power may nonetheless erode some of the most fundamental sources of U.S. power. [Japan] . . . challenges the economic competitiveness of many of the United States' most strategic industries, . . . it also undermines U.S. confidence and highlights U.S. weakness by throwing into sharp relief the country's most glaring domestic policy failures, such as its inability to educate its workforce adequately or to save enough to invest for its future economy (Dam et al. 1993: 29).

A Japanese author even sharpens the point of U.S.-Japan economic dispute as "political struggles for the defense of economic sovereignty" among capitalist nations (Kawasaki 1992: 267). The U.S.-Japan economic dispute is multifaceted with the issues of trading and market access to Japan, Japan's growing direct investment in the United States but limited success of foreign investment in Japan, macro-monetary polices, socioeconomic structural differences, and high-technology trade. All these affect the health of the military alliance in its security-related technology development and defense burden-sharing (Donnelly 1993: 335).

American politicians and economists understand that Japan is only the external factor to be blamed, and the U.S. domestic economy has a key role in balancing the U.S.-Japanese economic relationship. In the mid-1990s, U.S. companies went through radical changes in downsizing, raising productivity, and lowering costs (*Economist,* Sept. 16, 1995: 3–4). American manufacturing has bounced back and services are on the verge of revival. Nevertheless, as the economy has become sounder, not all American workers benefit from it; some have suffered from the changes by losing jobs and receiving less income. In 1993, IBM announced 63,000 layoffs, Sears Roebuck 50,000, and Boeing 28,000, some of the largest layoffs between 1993 and 1998 (*U.S. News and World Report,* Jan. 22, 1996: 51). In 1996, layoff announcements rose 8.5 percent over the previous year to total 477,147 (Internet Dallas Morning News, Jan. 9, 1997). In early 1998, the United States was ranked first in economic competitiveness in the world; at the same time, the number of U.S. business bankruptcy filings (54,027) in 1997 was still much higher than that in Japan (17,439) (*New York Times,* April 21, 1998: A6). Above all, the traditional economic frictions remain in the U.S.-Japan relationship.

Domestic political and economic climates indicate that official

U.S. security commitments to the alliance with Japan may continue to be redirected by U.S. government structure, public opinions, and economic difficulties. The U.S. defense industry, for example, has been in a constant state of competition with Japan, as discussed in the next section.

THE IMBALANCE OF MILITARY POWER

Realists and neorealists have argued that power and the distribution of power would determine national behavior and the occurrence of international conflicts. This section starts with an analysis of military power of both Japan and the United States and examines its impact on the two countries' behavior.

There is a general agreement that the United States remains the sole military hegemon in the world in the 1990s. As of mid-1990s, the total U.S. armed forces had about 1.5 million personnel. Directly relevant to the Asia-Pacific region is the United States Pacific Command (USPA-COM), headquartered in Hawaii with U.S. troops stationed in Alaska, Hawaii, Japan, South Korea, Singapore, Guam, Australia, and other areas. The Pacific Fleet (headquartered in Pearl Harbor) includes the Third Fleet and Seventh Fleet. The Seventh Fleet, headquartered in Yokosuka, Japan, covers the Western Pacific, Japan, the Philippines, ANZUS, and the Indian Ocean.

At present, the U.S. military power not only can overwhelm Japan, but also protects Japan's national security. From a realist view, the U.S. power position vis-à-vis Japan is a strategic paradox.

As of 1997, Japan's total active armed forces had 235,600 personnel with 46,700 reserves. The following are main segments of Japan's military power:

- Army (Ground Self-Defense Force): 147,700 personnel. Main battle tanks: some 1,110, including some 870 Type-74 and some 140 Type-90. Armored personnel carriers: some 900. Towed artillery: some 490. Surface-to-surface missiles: some 70 Type-88 coastal. Surface-to-air missiles: 320 Stinger, some 60 Type 81, some 80 Type 91, some 30 Type 93, and some 200 I HAWK. Attack helicopters: some 90 AH-1S.
- Navy (Maritime Self-Defense Force): 42,500 personnel. Principal surface combatants: 58, including 10 destroyers and 48 frigates.

      Submarines: 16. Mine warfare ships: 35. Amphibious vehicles: 66. Patrol and coastal combatants: 6.

- Air Force (Air Self-Defense Force): 44,100 personnel. Fighter Ground Attack (FGA): 2 squadron with 50 F-1; 1 squadron with 20 F-4EJ. Fighters: 10 squadron, 8 with 179 F-15J/DJ, 2 with 49 F-4EJ. Airborne Early Warning (AEW): 1 squadron with 10 E-2C. Air defense forces include 120 patriot missiles.
- U.S. Forces in Japan: 36,530 personnel. Army: 1,530 personnel; Navy: 6,700 personnel with the seventh Fleet headquartered in Yokosuka; Marines: 14,300 personnel; Air Force: 14,000 personnel with F-15C/D, F-16, etc. (*Military Balance* 1997–98: 182–183).

As discussed later, Japan has upgraded its capability and ensured its significant military power status in the Asia-Pacific region. What are the implications of the current and future trend of a military Japan? Will Japan change the military balance in the Asia-Pacific region and even terminate the U.S.-Japan alliance? Japan experts in the United States caution that "one of the root causes of global conflicts is fundamental shifts in the international balance of power," and the United States must work with Japan to avoid the conflicts (Dam et al. 1993: 33). One author suggests that the scenario for Japan as a regional military power would involve a continued arms procurement and require a reduced U.S. military presence in Asia (Chinworth 1992: 181).

George Friedman and Meredith Lebard further the power analysis and examine the U.S.-Japan relationship in a more alarming tone:

> [T]here are underlying reasons—economic, political, and military—that must put the United States and Japan on a collision course. Essentially, the issues are the same as they were in 1941. Japan needs to control access to its mineral supplies . . . [and] it must force the United States out of the western Pacific. As in the 1930s, both will engage in a cold war against each other which will, in extremes, spill over into a hot war (1991: 13–14).

Accordingly, the power distribution and shift may end the U.S.-Japan alliance. Of course, not all power analysts come to the same conclusion. From a realist balance-of-power perspective, another author wrote:

> Warning against possible American isolationism and the plausibility of a power vacuum being created by a dramatic withdrawal of the

US military from the region are, it must be said, more theoretical than practical. While a power vacuum is most unlikely, the candidates to fill it are either a revived Russian nationalist empire, an unstable militant China hostile to neighboring countries, or a nationalistic Japan without much confidence in its future economic prosperity. None of these are welcome, and this is precisely why the American military presence is necessary for the region's security. . . . [A] credible presence of US forward-deployed forces would be an effective counterbalance (Sasae 1994: 26).

This is to say that for the sake of a balance of power, the U.S.-Japan alliance has a reason to be maintained in order to contain either Japan or other new rising powers.

It is already evident through our discussion that the distribution-of-power analysis does not fully answer the question about the nature of the U.S.-Japan alliance and its future in the twenty-first century. Realists are not certain if it is the balance of power or the sole hegemony that favors stability and peace. Military capabilities aside, we should ask: how do the United States and Japan perceive each other? Do they intend to maintain or abandon the security treaty? How does the domestic situation play its role in the bilateral relationship? We have discussed these factors in earlier sections. Now we turn to elaborate how these factors have affected the functioning of the U.S.-Japan security alliance.

U.S.-JAPAN INTERACTION

The U.S.-Japan alliance remains sound in the 1990s, and the momentum for cooperation is stable in at least three regards: joint military production, joint military intelligence, and joint military missions.

With regard to joint military production in the 1990s, Japan produces four types of missiles under U.S. license: Sparrow, Sidewinder, Hawk, and Patriot. These missiles provide great deterrence against foreign attack. In the area of C^3I, Japan's technological advances become more integrated with and benefit from the U.S. system (Katzenstein and Okawara 1993b: 150–151). According to Japan's fleet commander Seiji Saeki, through high-level joint training exercises such as RIMPAC, Japan can make use of the U.S. Navy's evaluation system and thereby grasp its own present capabilities and weaknesses (FBIS-JST, June 3 1997: 46). At the same time, since 1993, the United States and Japan have been probing Theater Missile Defense (TMD), a system that would provide upper- and lower-tier defense against ballistic missile attacks, based on a combination of Aegis cruisers at sea, Airborne Warning and Control System (AWACS) in the air, and surface-to-air missiles on land (O'Hanlon 1997: 180). As many modern weapons are built under the U.S. license, Japan's technological thrust enjoys the American input and support.

On the cutting edge is the Japanese purchase/coproduction of FS-X fighters (F-2)—up to 141 by 2005. The FS-X is developed based on the Lockheed Martin F-16C and contracted by Mitsubishi Heavy Industries (MHI). Joint production aside, this collaboration proves a crucial technology transfer to Japan (*Jane's Defense Weekly,* Oct. 21, 1995: 4). The FS-X case, however, is also one recent indicator of the uneven road of U.S.-Japan military technological cooperation since the end of World War II. In the 1980s, Japan vehemently pursued an indigenous production of FS-X (F-2), and the autonomous defense policy collided with the principle of U.S.-Japan alliance. But Japan eventually abandoned the original plan for an independent production, which implied that its commitment to alliance is stronger than that to domestic defense industry (Green 1995: 124).

Extensive intelligence exchange has been a tradition since the Cold War era between the United States and Japan. Japan, for example, frequently received signal intelligence and satellite photographs from the United States. It greatly depends on the input of the U.S. intelligence and is meanwhile upgrading its own intelligence-gathering capabilities. In April 1997, Japan's Cabinet Legislation Bureau revealed that the Japanese military has for years carried out intelligence-collecting activities and shared military information with the United States in support of the latter's use of its armed forces (*Asahi Shimbun,* Apr. 12, 1997: 2). The United States is particularly supportive of Japan's efforts to bring civilians and military professionals into more efficient work, because Japan's capability will also increase American sources of intelligence in East Asia (Katzenstein and Okawara 1993b: 152–153).

As joint military missions, in addition to the US$13 billion aid to the 1991 Gulf War, the SDF ships were sent to the Gulf in April after the end of the war, and the JDA for the first time approved the refueling of U.S. ships by Japanese ships in the Gulf. Refueling was common in U.S.-Japan military exercises, but refueling for external purposes did not occur until 1991. In 1992, Japan dispatched troops to Cambodia to join the United States and other countries' troops for UN peacekeeping operations. In March 1996, the U.S. aircraft carrier *Independence* was sent from Japan to the Taiwan Strait area, monitoring the military crisis. It also was reported that the TMD in Japan would prevent missile attacks from

North Korea or China (*Jane's Defense Weekly,* Aug. 26, 1995: 14; *Defense News,* Apr. 22–28, 1996: 12, 26). Thus, traditional Japanese "defensive defense" is quietly giving way to "offensive defense" in favor of the U.S.-Japan security alliance. In early 1998, the United States and Japan launched the Bilateral Planning Committee (BPC) to put into force the revised U.S.-Japan Defense Cooperation Guidelines. The BPC is supervised by top security officials in both countries (Internet FBIS-EAS, Jan. 21, 1998).

The U.S.-Japanese security relationship is not problem-free, but coupled with, for example, technological competition that could undermine the foundation of the alliance (Green 1995). It is known that Japan is advanced in many civilian technology areas. As the line between military and nonmilitary technology is becoming so delicate, Japan has become a potential leading weapons producer. In essence, Japan has one economy that serves both civilian and military consumers. For that purpose, Japan has strategically used "international cooperation" with the United States (Samuels 1994: 320, 326–329).

In the early 1990s, Japan led the United States in five of the twenty critical technologies: semi-conductor materials and micro-electronic circuits, simulation and modeling, photonics, super-conductivity, and biotechnology. "With its rapid move to the frontiers of civilian high-technology industries Japan has become, in a non-traditional sense, a major military power, mostly without a conscious plan" (Katzenstein and Okawara 1993b: 150, 154). Thus, during the long process of technological competition, technology transfer has never been smooth, but exposed the lasting technological warfare. "Japanese technological advances were viewed as a threat to the U.S. industrial base, particularly the defense industry, which could undermine national security" (Keddell 1993: 160; Lorell 1995).

Also, the military base problem is far from resolved. The United States returned the Futenma Marine Air Station to Okinawans in April 1996. But due to the local opposition, Tokyo resisted the U.S. proposal for a heliport constructed in Marine Camp Schwab, located in central Okinawa, or a mobile offshore base. Tokyo rather preferred a so-called steel carpet—a pier-like steel structure fixed to the seabed. According a U.S. official, this option was to avoid a permanent U.S. construction (*Defense News,* Jan. 20–26, 1997: 12). In April 1997, Prime Minister Hashimoto had to issue special legislation to avoid the illegal use of land by the U.S. troops in Okinawa at the juncture of the expiration of the land lease. Since many Okinawans are anti-war, the future for the U.S. use of land is still unpredictable (Mochizuki 1997: 25–26).

The U.S.-Japan defense cooperation encountered another major obstacle in 1997 as Japan withdrew from a joint TMD project. After three years of discussion, Tokyo decided against participating in this missile project out of the fear of offending China and overspending military sources. American officials concluded that Japan was simply not ready for a project that could cost it US$10 billion a year—more than one-fourth of its current US$35 billion military budget—for four or five years to come. The Japanese military establishment opposed this joint project with the United States because it would not have funds for other defense priorities. It was reported that the JDA decided to postpone its participation for a year and to continue with further study (Internet FBIS-EAS, July 8, 1997).

Security issues aside, after a few years of silence, economic disputes came back on the top agenda of U.S.-Japan summits in 1997. The Clinton administration warned against the possible expansion of Japan's trade surplus. An American official said that "America's ultimate goal is to sustain its economic edge in dealing with Japan in order to enhance U.S. national interests." The tough economic approach was coupled with rekindled criticisms of Japan in the U.S. Congress (*Nihon Keizai Shimbun,* Apr. 22, 1997: 5). In a meeting with Prime Minister Hashimoto in June, President Clinton cited a prediction that the U.S. trade deficit with Japan could increase to US$130 billion in two years from its current US$35.5 billion. The Japanese were told that Clinton's figure was the current account deficit, not just the merchandise trade deficit. The current account balance is the broadest measure of trade covering the flow of goods and service, as well as investment income and other monetary transfers (Internet FBIS-EAS, June 24, 1997). In October, due to the U.S. demand of equal rights for U.S. shippers in Japan, to match those for Japanese shippers in the United States, the Federal Maritime Commission was close to directing the Coast Guard to turn away Japanese cargo ships headed into any U.S. port (Internet New York Times, Oct. 17, 1997).

In 1998, the faltering Japanese economy generated a subtle political tension between Washington and Tokyo. In Japan, Secretary Albright said that "I understand that Japan sometimes feels it is being pushed too hard and too fast to take steps that would be difficult even in the best of times." She added that "I hope you understand that the concerns Americans have expressed are those of a good friend and staunch ally who wishes you well" (*Washington Post,* Apr. 29, 1998: 28).

In the current U.S.-Japan alliance, perceptions and domestic factors play a major role. Officials from both countries have reached a consensus on the necessity of greater military cooperation and perceived the alliance as a cornerstone of Asia-Pacific security—with or without any country as a concrete threat. The two countries' leaders perceive their common interests not only in the military, but also broadly in economics, the natural environment, the UN system, the WTO, and other global issues (FBIS-EAS, Apr. 18, 1996: 1–3). Official views seem to have overwhelmed resistant voices from both countries' domestic elements. And the prevailing official attitude is predominant, at least for now, in consolidating the viability of the military alliance.

Domestic restraints remain strong and powerful, however. They could favor or oppose government foreign policy, and their unpredicted eruption could totally change the nature of the military alliance. The U.S.-Japan alliance will face serious tests in future international crises.

In balance, the U.S.-Japan alliance will be featured by the following points. First, the United States will continue to be the guarantor of Japan's security, as Asian nations are still suspicious of Japan as a regional military power (see table 3.3). The U.S.-Japan security alliance offers Japan considerable flexibility in buffering pressure on its military buildup that would jeopardize its relations with neighboring countries, especially China and Korea. With the release of the U.S.-Japan Defense Cooperation Guidelines in New York, the ASEAN ministers met and urged Japanese foreign minister Keizo Obuchi to continue Japan's military transparency. South Korea also expressed its suspicion of Japan's future military role despite the guidelines' declared target against North Korea (Internet FBIS-EAS, Sept. 25, 1997).

Second, for some time to come, official opinions in both Japan and

---

TABLE 3.3

How Asia Perceives Japan

Has Japan come to be trusted by Asia?			Would Japan become a military power that made its neighbors	
	Yes (percent)	No (percent)	feel threatened?	Yes (percent)
Bangkok	79		Thailand	34
Beijing		85		
Jakarta	85		Malaysia	38
Manila	55			
Seoul		61	Singapore	36
Singapore	62			
Shanghai		79		

Source: Peter Jennings, "Strategic Outlook," Asia-Pacific Defense Reporter (March–April 1996): 7; Internet Nation (Thailand), April 25, 1997.

the United States will favor the existence of the bilateral alliance, and consequent government policies will keep the alliance moving on track. Washington and Tokyo will be able to keep opposing forces at bay, at least in the near future.

Third, despite the confirmation of a U.S.-Japan alliance in 1996 and the review of Defense Cooperation Guidelines in 1997, the changing distribution of power and domestic factors could create an uncertain alliance. The overall trend has been that Japan tends to be more independent, the U.S. military forces have gradually withdrawn from East Asia, and the U.S.-Japan alliance is shifting toward a new destiny.

SUMMARY

This chapter demonstrates that elite perception in Washington and Tokyo is a far more important factor than domestic situation and the distribution of power in the security relationship. It has been and will be up to the decision makers to decide if they want to maintain the military alliance. Despite all the challenges, the two governments have reached a consensus to maintain a strong security commitment for a foreseeable future.

It has become increasingly clear that China is a major third party between the United States and Japan. In redefining the alliance, both countries evidently have China in mind. The Taiwan issue, a potential Korean crisis, and disputes over the South China Sea islands all have become new concerns for the U.S.-Japan security alliance. Yet, the United States and Japan are not necessarily moving toward the policy of containing China; rather, they have emphasized the significance of engaging and cooperating with China. In the future, the China factor will only become more tangible in influencing both the U.S.-Japan alliance and the entire Asia-Pacific security.

4

The Balance of Power between China and Japan: Growth and/or Mutual Threat?

In this chapter, we examine the last part of the triad—Sino-Japanese relations—by focusing on its military dimension. For nearly five decades after World War II, military security was not an important measure for Sino-Japanese relations. The reason, as Akira Iriye suggested, was that the security tie between the two countries had never been "purely bilateral but aspects of larger patterns and developments" (Iriye 1990: 624). In other words, China and Japan did not have any direct military cooperation or confrontation during that period of time.

Since the end of the Cold War, however, the international system has transformed rapidly. So has the Sino-Japanese military relationship. Direct and bilateral military contacts between the two countries seem to be inevitable in the 1990s, despite the continued U.S.-Japan security alliance. At the core is the military buildup in both China and Japan, which has caused mutual concern and unprecedentedly explicit military-related reactions. This chapter will take a close look at the initial development of the new Sino-Japanese security relationship.

MUTUAL PERCEPTIONS

Japan

We begin with Japan's new assessment of international security and the possible security means it may apply at the end of the twentieth century:

> [D]iplomatic and domestic efforts alone cannot always prevent armed aggression from foreign countries. Nor can they actually resist aggression if it has occurred. Defense capability, as an expression of intention and capability of resisting aggression, has functions of preventing aggression and resisting it when it occurs. In this sense, the functions of defense power cannot be substituted by any other means and thus are the last resort in the defense of national peace and security (JDA 1996: 57).

The end of the Cold War has complex implications for Japan. First of all, the Soviet Union, a longtime major potential threat, collapsed and declined, and left Japan with much more relaxed northern borders. At the same time, China emerged as a great economic and military power in East Asia, and naturally, Japan focused attention on China. While rethinking China, many Japanese scholars and analysts have tended to view it as a threat. The Japanese government view was initially optimistic and calm but became more outspoken and critical, and, therefore, more similar to non-official perceptions, especially after 1994. Between 1994 and 1996, the Japanese were preoccupied with disputes with China over Taiwan, nuclear tests, and Senkaku/Diaoyu islands.

During much of the twentieth century, China perceived Japan from a perspective of Chinese cultural superiority, and Japan perceived China from the perspective of the Japanese economic advancement. This pattern of perception was coupled with Chinese hatred of Japan and Japanese guilt over its atrocities in China during World War II (Ijiri 1990). This mental complex underlay the two countries' mutual perceptions until the late 1980s, but no longer function exactly the same way, as we will discuss.

In the early 1990s, some Japanese scholars envisioned that China's enhanced military capability, highlighted by its renewed claims over disputed territories, was evidence of emerging Chinese hegemony and its ambition to fill the power vacuums left from the Cold War. China was seen as a power seeking to destabilize or overthrow the existing order (Kasahara 1992; Hiramatsu 1992; Hironaka 1994). One author warned that "China appears ready to protect by force its own territorial interests, a move that could create new tensions with Japan and other Asian countries in the future" (Nishihara 1993: 92). Another author echoed that the only point Japan had to watch in Asia was Chinese expansionism and that a Sino-U.S. dispute would be the most important factor among East Asian security problems (Kasahara 1994). For these analysts, if China is not considered a threat, it is at least a potential threat (Tanaka 1994: 43). Several specific issues concerned Japan: Beijing's political succession, its attempt for a blue-water navy, and the Diaoyu/Senkaku Islands dispute between the two countries.

By the mid-1990s, Japanese scholars consolidated their negative views of China through new events. A professor at Rikkyo University argued that China's nuclear tests displayed its "power diplomacy" and China's emphasis on sovereignty meant its indifference in cooperating with other countries (FBIS-EAS, Apr. 19, 1996: 18). Ko Maruyama of the Defense Research Center in Japan said in May 1996 that China would use military force over territorial issues such as Senkaku and Taiwan. He urged the Japanese government to prepare to respond to emergency situations (FBIS-EAS, May 10, 1996: 11–12). Masashi Nishihara of the National Institute for Defense Studies in Tokyo suggested that "Japan would discourage, and if necessary, deter a politically and militarily, if not economically, dominant China" (Nishihara 1996: 175). Nishihara made it clear that Japan would not deal with China by itself but through the support of U.S. moves to check China if it became aggressive on security issues such as Taiwan. This view was also advocated by other Japanese experts. They noted that China has been upgrading its naval and air forces through purchasing Russia's most advanced fighters and warships. China's formidable forces have occupied the Spratly Islands and consolidated its operational activities in the South China Sea area, and consequently stimulated anxiety among the concerned nations. Moreover, China has not disavowed the possible use of force against Taiwan. "Because only the deterrence capabilities of the United States can respond effectively to Chinese tendencies, maintaining America's presence in East Asia is critical to regional peace and stability" (Morimoto 1997: 92).

Not all Japanese analysts, of course, agree to the arguments about the "China threat." One author noted that while China is upgrading its naval capabilities, it is far from being able to have invasion power (Tsukamoto 1990). In China's new security concept, some authors noted, Chinese leaders attach importance to non-military means for security by activating domestic support for the Communist Party, maintaining economic growth, and stabilizing the external environment (Kasahara 1990).

Ikuo Kayahara of the National Institute for Defense Studies called for a sober examination of the "China threat." From strategic and economic perspectives, the author concluded, the "China threat" is exaggerated and the estimates are over-inflated. He expected that the PRC would play a positive role in a new world order although he encouraged China to increase its transparency in military activities (1994). As an author put it, "the view in Tokyo is moderately optimistic about the future bilateral relations" (Akaha 1993: 100). Some argued that both Japan and the United States should engage China in reaching constructive views on the regional security. Even if China does not accept the U.S.-Japan Security Treaty "as a public good at this time, the United States and Japan should encourage it to participate in creating a common security order" in the Asia-Pacific region (Takahashi 1997: 127).

These scholars' perceptions are comparable to official government views. Relatively speaking, the Japanese official view of China is more balanced and forward-looking. Kenzo Oshima, minister of political affairs of the Japanese Embassy in Washington, was inclined to engage rather than isolate China in international affairs and expected a more democratic China in the future (Oshima 1992: 61). Former ambassador to Beijing (1984–1987) Yosuke Nakae stated: "It is certain that without friendly and cooperative relations between Japan and China there can be no support for peace, stability, or prosperity in Asia" (see Arase 1993: 123). The Japan Defense Agency desired to "build relations of trust" with China and other countries in the Post Cold War era (FBIS-EAS, Jan. 6, 1995: 5). Its White Paper "Defense of Japan 1994" stated that Beijing's top priority was economic growth, and Chinese military modernization could only proceed gradually (JDA 1994). A Japanese official offered a detailed study in this regard:

> [T]o the extent that China sees its strategic environment as favorable and non-confrontational, especially as it relates to the US, Russia and Japan, there should be no strategic reason for China drastically to alter the course it has pursued so far, other than to make tactical adjustments to balance economic reform and domestic stability (Sasae 1994: 11).

Official Japanese views, however, have tended to be more critical of China since 1994. On China's nuclear testing in May 1995, Japan called it "extremely regrettable" (Internet MOFA, May 15, 1995). When China conducted another nuclear test in August, Japan stated that "China's nuclear testing today is regrettable also from the viewpoint of the ODA (official development aid) Charter. Japan will have to cope with its future economic cooperation with China restrainedly" (Internet MOFA, Aug. 17, 1995). In June 1996, Japan expressed a similar "regrettable" attitude but did not mention economic sanctions when China conducted a nuclear test (Internet MOFA, June 8, 1996). In May 1996, Prime Minister Ryutaro Hashimoto renewed Japanese territorial claims to the disputed Senkaku islands (FBIS-EAS, May 10, 1996: 12). LDP secretary general Koichi Kato warned that "China's missile testing in international waters in the Taiwan Strait was behavior that cannot be tolerated" (*Far Eastern Economic Review,* Aug. 15, 1996: 28).

The 1996 JDA White Paper "Defense of Japan" stated that "we need to continue to watch Chinese actions, such as modernization of its nuclear, naval and air forces; expanding its scope of activities in the high seas; and growing tension in the Taiwan Strait caused by its military exercises" (JDA 1996: 45). In early 1997, Naoaki Murata, administrative vice minister of the JDA, voiced his concern: "Chinese defense expenditure has grown by more than 10 percent annually over the past eight years and will continue to grow at a rate of greater than 10 percent in fiscal 1997." He said that Tokyo needs to monitor Chinese military moves given the lack of transparency in the country's defense spending, which was US$9.7 billion for 1997 according to Beijing's announcement (Internet FBIS-EAS, Mar. 5, 1997).

Japan's alertness about China is also visible from the perspective of Sino-U.S. relations. Japan does not anticipate a U.S.-Chinese alliance against itself. Tokyo has noticed, however, that there is a competition of influence between itself and the United States in China. China has a lot more to learn and receive from the United States than from Japan, such as a legal system and the telecommunications market. Some Japanese believe that Americans have overall and long-term strategies toward China, whereas Japanese businesses only seek cheap labor in China and have no important proposals (FBIS-EAS, Jan. 10, 1995: 10). Within this strategic triangle, a Japanese official wrote that "ideally for Japan, Japan-US relations should be excellent, Japan-China relations good, and US-China relations reasonably good" (Sasae 1994: 12).

The fact is that China wants to get as much as possible from both the United States and Japan. But Japan is worried about U.S. diplomatic initiatives toward China. Japan wants a stable triangle despite its suspicion about China. In August 1997, before his trip to China, Prime Minister Hashimoto outlined four points to better Japan-China relations: deepening mutual understanding, expanding dialogue, promoting cooperation, and creating common order (Internet FBIS-EAS, Aug. 29, 1997). In his long speech on Japan's China policy made to the Yomiuri International Economic Society on August 28, Prime Minister Hashimoto said that China will not pose a threat to other countries and invited China to form a common order for Asia and the world. Hashimoto elaborated the fields in which the two countries can work together: environment, energy, trade, finance, investment, and political security (Internet FBIS-EAS, Sept. 8, 1997). Visiting China in September, Prime Minister Hashimoto said to an audience of 800 Chinese academics, government officials, and other personnel that the two countries should establish "a constructive partnership" (Internet FBIS-EAS Sept. 8, 1997). He summarized the forthcoming Japan-U.S. Defense Cooperation Guidelines and interpreted "areas surrounding Japan" as a situation rather than a geographic concept. He further urged Chinese leaders to conduct frank security discussions with Japan. Hashimoto acknowledged that Chinese leaders understood his explanation of "areas surrounding Japan" but did not agree with him (Internet FBIS-EAS, Sept. 15, 1997).

As we see, in late 1997, Japan developed new views of building better relations with China, partially as a response to the improved Sino-U.S. relationship. Criticism of China from 1994 to 1996 yielded to more positive statements after 1997.

The implicit intention of containing China aside, the official view in Japan holds that Tokyo should continue to seek to incorporate China as a responsible participant in the Asia-Pacific security mechanism and to encourage Beijing to abide by international norms. Prime Minister Hashimoto said to a news conference that "the building of friendly and stable relations among Japan, the United States, and China is indispensable." In order to eliminate China's concern about the guidelines, Hashimoto said that Tokyo will continue to make efforts during security dialogue and direct exchanges between defense officials of the two countries (Internet FBIS-EAS Sept. 9, 1997). Some Japanese officials have supported a proposal for a trilateral security dialogue between Japan, China, and the United States (Garrett and Glaser 1996: 20–21).

China

The consensus in China is that Japan is a "potential" threat, but the two countries should maintain a stable relationship. In the early 1990s, Chinese scholars and analysts were aware of Japan's military expansion, including its upgrading of combat aircraft and ships, the passage of the legislation on troop dispatch abroad, and the ongoing debate on a new constitution that would grant Japan greater freedom in its military operations. Chinese observers believed that Japan was seeking a more active role in the international arena (Ge 1989; S. Huang 1990; Chang 1992). "Japan has become more active and independent in conducting its foreign policy in an attempt to fill the vacancy in the Asia-Pacific region left by the withdrawal of U.S. and Russian influences" (Lin 1992: 10). Toward Japan's efforts for a greater power status in Asia and in the world, such as a permanent membership in the UN Security Council, Chinese leaders or analysts often took cautious or discouraging views. Some analysts even ridiculed Japan's new great power policy (Z. Huang 1990).

Two military analysts wrote that Japan had not correctly understood and thoroughly apologized for its atrocities inflicted upon Asian nations in history; because of that, it would not be able to establish a good image in Asia. The two authors commented that some Japanese China experts refused to acknowledge and even asked Asian victims not to discuss the history of Japanese aggression. According to the Chinese analysts, this kind of Japanese mentality revealed Japan's dishonesty and caused doubt about its future behavior (Han and Song 1994: 152–153).

Despite the worry about Japan's remilitarization, Chinese Japan specialists believed that the rise of Japanese militarism is "one possibility, not an inevitable development." This view was a key tone in the late 1980s and early 1990s. They believed that Japan would stand by its traditional Yoshida Doctrine by placing economic development rather than military buildup at the foundation of its foreign policy. As one author analyzed, it seemed impossible that Japan would become a major military power by the end of this century. Japan as a military giant would cause strong opposition from the international society and from Japan itself. In that case, Japan would be put under nuclear deterrence from China; the United States and Western Europe would not support a nuclear Japan. Therefore, Japan would not become a major military power but rather remain primarily dependent on U.S. protection (Rong 1987: 72).

As one Chinese author wrote, Sino-Japanese relations as a whole had made progress. The essence of existing problems between the two countries was how to handle the history of Japanese invasion and relations with Taiwan (Lin 1992: 308). China needed loans, investment, and advanced technology from Japan; the Chinese also understood that Japan relied on China's endorsement for its great power status. Japan desired permanent membership in the UN Security Council, cooperation with

China on its Asia policy, and the Chinese market for Japanese goods. Chinese scholars believed that it was natural for Japan to be a great political power. But as a whole, the Chinese welcomed Japan as an economic and peaceful power rather than a military power (Feng 1994: 114, 116–117). A Chinese scholar offered Japan the following policy advice:

> For Japan to become a world political power, it must first become an Asian political power. To become an Asian political power, Japan must be so recognized by China. . . . [S]olid advancement of Japanese-Chinese relations will be beneficial not only to the two countries but to the peace and development of the whole Asia Pacific region (Zhou 1993: 196).

Chinese public image of Japan became more pointed and critical in the mid-1990s. China saw Prime Minister Hashimoto's visit to the Yasukuni Shrine in July 1996 as a dangerous move and a signal of the rising Japanese militarism. Some Japan experts in China also perceived the Japan threat over disputed territories and urged Beijing to take military actions in defense of Diaoyu islands. Moreover, many Chinese believed that Japan would split China and support Taiwan's independence (Zi and Xiao 1997: 251–295). An article in *China Daily* called the U.S.-Japan pact more harmful than good for Asia (May 23, 1996: 4). Another article in *Beijing Review* noted that "a major thrust of the reassessment involved shifting the focus of the U.S.-Japanese security treaty from defending Japan to maintaining security for the Asia-Pacific region. Essentially, this means Japan will turn from a protected to a protecting party in the alliance" (Ni 1996: 8–9).

As Japan is rising up to the status of a great economic and political power, Chinese analysts are especially alarmed by its formidable military strength. According to them, in the 50 years since World War II, Japan has quietly revitalized its armed forces; increased its defense expenditure; modernized its weaponry with high technology; and established independent land, naval, and air forces. Further, as an expert displayed, Japan has become a potential great nuclear-missile power—with most advanced rocket systems convertible for missiles of various ranges. As a result, the strength of Japan's Self-Defense Forces has grown far beyond the scope of national defense and once again rung the alarm bell. In this regard, Chinese analysts openly identify Japan as a threat: Japan has again become a big military power and the world must be vigilant (Zi and Xiao 1997: 78, 86; S. Zheng 1996: 74–77).

After the 1989 Tiananmen incident, meeting with a Japanese guest,

Deng Xiaoping reiterated: "No matter what has changed internationally, or what has changed domestically in Japan and China, the Sino-Japanese friendship shouldn't change, or cannot change" (*Renmin Ribao,* Sept. 20, 1989). Since 1994, however, corresponding to the deteriorating Japanese view of China, Chinese official perception of Japan has shifted more negatively and closer to the Chinese public opinion. In October 1994, Beijing expressed strong displeasure over Japan's decision allowing the Taiwanese vice premier Hsu Li-teh to attend the XII Asian Games in Hiroshima. A Chinese official noted that when Japan examines the post-Cold War Asian security environment, its target is China; the Japan-U.S. alliance in 1996 treated North Korea, Russia, and China as potential threats (D. Zhang 1996: 26, 29). Chinese Foreign Ministry spokesman Shen Guofang warned that when Japan and the United States revised their national defense policy, it should safeguard, not damage, stability in the region (FBIS-CHI, Nov. 8, 1995: 1). Beijing contends that, contrary to the theory of China threat, the real threat would come from Japan and the United States (*Beijing Review,* Nov. 11–17, 1996: 8–9).

Before and after the release of the Japan-U.S. Defense Cooperation Guidelines in September 1997, Chinese officials and leaders expressed great displeasure and suspicion. *Ta Kung Pao,* a newspaper in Hong Kong with strong official affiliation in Beijing, made some clear points. Its editorial stated that the guidelines would infringe upon China's sovereignty whether the Taiwan Strait is included in the scope of Japan-U.S. cooperation directly or indirectly. "It is unusual to use such a vague expression [about the concept of areas surrounding Japan] in a serious political document" (Sept. 25, 1997: 2).

Xu Xin, former deputy chief of the General Staff of the PLA and former director of the China Institute for International Strategic Studies (CIISS), told a reporter that China has become the target of the new guidelines, which contain some intention of aggression. He added that a judgment on the guidelines needs more time (Internet FBIS-CHI, Oct. 3, 1997). Chinese foreign minister Qian made a point that strengthening mutual reliance among concerned countries to maintain regional stability is more important than expanding military alliance (Internet FBIS-EAS, July 21, 1997). Chinese Foreign Ministry spokesman Shen Guofang cautioned that the guidelines review "should not pose a threat to the Asian region and other countries" (Internet FBIS-EAS, Aug. 13, 1997). It is interesting to note that the Chinese criticism of the guidelines has been low-profiled. Conceivably, Chinese leaders decided not to strongly oppose the guidelines review because of its uncertain feature.

As a focus of their analysis of Japan, both Chinese analysts and officials use history as a "mirror." They ask "Where will Japan go?" when they believe that Japan is trying to "shirk responsibility" for World War II. As the second largest economy in the world, they argue, Japan is able to turn its superb industrial technology into military use at any time (Da 1995: 4–5). Articles of the official Chinese newspaper *People's Daily* urged Japan to remember its aggressions in Asian nations while endorsing Prime Minister Murayama's personal apology (Aug. 16, 1995: 7; Aug. 31, 1995: 9). Two military analysts wrote that although Japan will not necessarily return to militarism, its ambiguous attitude toward the World War II history only causes suspicion by Asian nations (Han and Song 1994: 152). Visiting South Korea in November 1995, President Jiang Zemin joined President Kim Young Sam in warning of a military threat from Japan. In July 1997, Chinese defense minister Chi Haotian said to the visiting LDP delegation led by Secretary General Koichi Kato that there are always people in Japan who attempt to deny historical facts and confound black and white (Internet FBIS-CHI, July 18, 1997). In August, a *Xinhua* article urged people to "watch out for revival of Japanese militarism in new guise" (Internet FBIS-CHI, Aug. 18, 1997).

Still, when China looks at the U.S.-Japan-China triangle as a whole, it tends to describe it as a cooperative rather than a hostile structure. Analyst Chen Peiyao wrote that, in the short term, Japan and the United States will likely combine forces to contain China on certain issues. Most likely, however, the triangle will move toward being equilateral, interdependent, and cooperative (Chen 1995: 3–4). Former ambassador to the United States Zhu Qizhen wrote that Sino-U.S.-Japan relations are moving toward a new historical phase, but have not embarked on a healthy track. The triangle should become a new type of cooperative relationship. He saw Japan and the United States as allies, while Japan is trying to change its dependence on the United States and the United States is trying to maintain a dominant position. Sino-U.S. relations contain both conflict and cooperation. Sino-Japanese relations have a good foundation and it should be maintained. Zhu highlighted Taiwan as the most sensitive issue for the triangular relationship (Zhu 1995). It was reported that Foreign Minister Qian expressed his interest in conducting unofficial trilateral talks among Chinese, Japanese, and American academic circles (Internet Japan MOFA, Oct. 1, 1997).

In sum, Sino-Japanese mutual perceptions have at least two outstanding features. First, entering the 1990s, both countries increasingly perceived each other as threats. The threat, however, is perceived only as potential and precautionary. The two countries have not reached a consensus or a conclusion of such a threat. Second, the mutual perceptions tend to be relaxed and positive when the two sides place their bilateral relationship within the Sino-Japanese-U.S. triangle. It appears that both countries expect the United States to be a fair broker.

DOMESTIC CONSTRAINTS

Japan

After World War II, Japan's domestic social forces exercised great impact on the making of its China policy. The most influential factors included public opinion, various opposition parties, business interests, the bureaucracy, and the LDP (Mendl 1978: 45–52). Before Japan and China formalized their diplomatic relationship in 1978, these factors had played various roles in Japan's China policy.

Public opinion, surveyed through opinion polls, could set limits and restraints on the China policymaking. Popular feelings had occasionally large effects on the government; the public, for example, contributed to the improved and normalized Sino-Japanese relations in the early 1970s. But an occurrence as such was rare, and policy decisions mostly were not made in response to public demands.

Opposition parties often leaned toward Beijing to a certain extent. Their role, however, was weakened by divisions between and within the parties. For example, the Japan Socialist Party (JSP; later renamed the Social Democratic Party—SDP), the largest opposition party, disputed among its own factions.

Business groups focused on economic and commercial interests and strove for competitive standing. Business leaders did not exert persistent pressure on the authorities to develop relations with China, partly because the Japanese economy was closely tied to the United States, at least until the late 1970s.

Bureaucratic rivalries underscored their own differences over China policy. Each ministry and bureau competed to implement a particular policy. Still, there was a mainstream opinion, which favored Taiwan over China for almost three decades, despite the wide appeal for an enhanced relationship with China.

The LDP as the core of Japanese leadership opposed formal recognition of China, but also displayed peculiar characteristics in handling China policy. The LDP took a "supra-partisan" stand on China through a compromise among all LDP factions and the opposition parties, but individual politicians might use China policy to strengthen their status within a faction or party. And the LDP tended to depend on the MOFA to formulate its China policy (Mendl 1978: 47).

That was history. Beijing-Tokyo diplomatic normalization was finally substituted for the old pattern of Sino-Japanese relations. Meanwhile, Japanese domestic politics continues its evolution. Japan's political party system and government leadership have undergone some unprecedented changes in the 1990s. For example, Japan swiftly elected five prime ministers from November 1991 to January 1996 (see table 4.1).

The major event was the July 1993 election. Before the election, the Hata-Ozawa and another group of LDP members left the party to form respectively the Shinsei (New Life) Party and the Sakigake (Harbinger) Party. As a result, the LDP lost its majority in the lower house although it remained the largest party (Abe, Shindo, and Kawato 1994: 122–123). It was also expected that a coalition government would not last long, as indicated in table 4.1. In June 1994, the SDP sent its person as prime minister and broke the chain of the consecutive selection by the LDP. But within two years, the LDP's Hashimoto won back the prime ministership and somewhat restored the old political stage.

Underneath the transformation of the party system, the domestic factors that had traditionally affected Japan's China policy have exhibited new images. First of all, Prime Minister Hashimoto is a representative of the post-Cold War politicians, and the 1996 coalition government was composed of three-quarter first-time cabinet members (*Renmin Ribao,* Jan. 16, 1996: 6). It seemed that the new generation of Japanese leadership has removed some pro-Beijing factions. Prime Minister Hashimoto and the opposition New Frontier Party (NFP) president Ichiro Ozawa were both from the Tanaka faction of the LDP, but did not have the similar feeling and political experience with China that former prime minister Kakuei

TABLE 4.1
Turnovers of Prime Ministers

Prime Minister	Start of Term	End of Term
Kiichi Miyazawa	November 5, 1991	August 6, 1993
Morihiro Hosokawa	August 6, 1993	April 25, 1994
Tsutomu Hata	April 25, 1994	June 29, 1994
Tomiichi Murayama	June 29, 1994	January 11, 1996
Ryutaro Hashimoto	January 11, 1996	July 13, 1998

TABLE 4.2
Japanese Diet, January 1998

Parties/Coalitions	HR	HC
Government Coalition	**276**	**143**
Liberal Democratic Party	259	119
Social Democratic Party	15	21
New Party Sakigake	2	3
Opposition Coalition I (Minyuren)	**99**	**41**
Democratic Party	53	17
Sun Party	10	3
From Five	3	3
Voice of the People	15	3
Yuai (Friendship and Love)	14	9
Democratic Reform Federation	2	3
Independents	2	3
Opposition Coalition II (Heiwa/Reform)	**46**	**3**
Heiwa	37	0
Reform Club	9	3
Others		
Liberal Party	42	12
Communist Party	26	14
Independents Club	2	0
Komei	0	25
Niin Club	0	4
New Socialist Party Alliance for Peace	0	3
Non-affiliation	8	7
Vacancy	1	0
Total	500	252

HR: House of Representatives; HC: House of Councilors
Source: Prepared by Ronald Montaperto and based on various sources.

Tanaka did. A statement (The Future of China in the Context of Asian Security) by conservative politicians in both LDP and NFP urged the government to admonish Chinese chauvinism in the South China Sea and Senkaku islands and to use economic means to influence Chinese behavior. Meanwhile, pro-Taiwan officials are regaining power in Tokyo (Green and Self 1996: 45). In August 1997, for example, Japan's chief cabinet secretary Seiroku Kajiyama openly proposed that the new Japan-U.S. Defense Cooperation Guidelines should cover emergencies in the Taiwan Strait and aroused strong criticisms from China (Internet FBIS-EAS, Aug. 21, 1997). Overall, Japanese officials have become more outspoken and assertive on China policy, notably in expressing their views and concerns about China's nuclear tests and military exercises over Taiwan (Numata 1996). The generation that contributed to the normalization of diplomatic ties has retired or died in both countries, leaving no channels for candid discussions (Internet FBIS-EAS, Mar. 25, 1997).

Opposition parties, such as the SDP, the public, and the media all have turned to be more critical of China in the mid-1990s. Secretary general of SDP Kanju Sato expressed his concerns over China's nuclear tests during an interview with Chinese premier Li Peng in July 1996 (FBIS-EAS, July 12, 1996: 10). Similarly, the Sakigake Party (one of the three ruling coalition parties) chief Masayoshi Takemura urged for China's early ending of nuclear tests and for restraining its behavior toward Taiwan (FBIS-CHI, July 11, 1996:4–5). In terms of public opinion, in January 1997, when asked "which region or country do you think may become a military threat to Japan," 39.1 percent of the Japanese public picked China (55 percent picked North Korea). When asked "do you think China will become a threat to the economy of Japan in the future," 73.6 percent said yes (*Yomiuri Shimbun,* Mar. 17, 1997: 16–17). The *Yomiuri Shimbun* and the long time left-wing *Asahi Shimbun* criticized China on nuclear tests and military exercises. An article in *Tokyo Ekonomisuto* argued that Prime Minister Hashimoto should not take a "considerate attitude" towards China. If he "appears too agreeable to China in word and deed, Japan-PRC affairs may unexpectedly become his Achilles' heel" (Internet FBIS-EAS, May 1, 1997). All domestic factors have appeared less favorable toward China than before.

Nevertheless, government officials, political parties, public opinion, and other domestic factors continue to be diversified social forces that constrain Japan's China policy. The SDP, for example, is more inclined to apologize to Asian nations for Japan's World War II aggression and to develop relations with China, whereas the LDP appears to be more nationalistic. Murayama apologized for Japan's atrocities during World War II, but Hashimoto paid a visit to the Yasukuni Shrine for the Japanese war dead and was reluctant to discuss the issue of Korean and other comfort women who served as sex slaves for the Japanese military.

It is also inevitable that different needs within the same political group have to compromise on issues concerning China. While the Hashimoto cabinet protested against China's nuclear tests, the same cabinet strongly supported China's early accession to the WTO (FBIS-EAS, July 23, 1996: 15). Whereas the JDA is increasingly worried about China's military capabilities after the Cold War, the MOFA chooses to improve relations with China. MOFA administrative vice minister Sadayuki Hayashi stated that "It cannot be said that the ratio of the country's defense spending to its national finance is particularly prominent compared with past fiscal years" (Internet FBIS-EAS, Mar. 10, 1997).

Even the 1997 JDA Defense White Paper had an adjusted tone. It noted Chinese military modernization shifting from quantity to quality in dealing with modern warfare, but concluded that China is placing top priority on its economic modernization and that its military power will increase at a moderate rate (Internet FBIS-EAS, July 8, 1997). Containment of China has been voiced by some Japanese officials in the 1990s, but the mainstream of Japanese elites has rejected this hawkish policy, as secretary general of the LDP Koichi Kato insisted (FBIS-EAS, July 24, 1996: 35–36). The Foreign Policy Guidelines issued by the LDP Foreign Affairs Committee stated that efforts should be made to convene a conference of the defense ministers of Japan, the United States, and China and to hold a Japan-U.S.-China summit meeting. The LDP report encouraged cooperation with China and proposed that China should be a new member of the G-7 summit (*Yomiuri Shimbun,* Apr. 11, 1997: 2).

Neither have newspapers became anti-China all at once. Viewing the improved Sino-U.S. relations in July 1996, *Asahi Shimbun* welcomed the upcoming Sino-U.S. high-level mutual visits and encouraged Japan to help China's membership with the WTO (FBIS-EAS, July 15, 1996: 12–13). In early 1997, *Nihon Keizai Shimbun* suggested that leaders of Japan and China should enhance personal ties and explore common interests in wide-ranging fields, including consultations between defense officials (Internet FBIS-EAS, Mar. 25, 1997). In July, *Gaiko Forum,* a monthly foreign policy journal in Tokyo, held a discussion between Chinese vice foreign minister Tang Jiaxuan and Japanese ambassador to China Yoshiyasu Sato in Beijing. The interview was used in commemoration of the twenty-fifth anniversary of the normalization of Japan-China relations. The two officials talked about history, international relations, and civilization (*Gaiko Forum,* Sept. 30, 1997: 24–35).

More importantly, Japan-China economic ties have become stronger, and Japanese business groups have become more supportive of friendly relations with China than before. Japan has been a major source of aid, loans, and credit to China in the 1990s. After the 1989 Tiananmen incident, Japanese business lobbied to lift sanctions and to resume aid to China. In 1996, Japan-bound goods accounted for 20.4 percent of China's total overseas sales. Japan-China trade was 20.7 percent of China's foreign trade total, reaching US$60.6 billion (*China Daily,* Mar. 6, 1997: 1).

As observed by many Japanese analysts, when Chinese wishes become known to the Japanese public, there is a great deal of enthusiasm and supportive reaction from the Japanese public. This was true in 1978 when China announced its goals to achieve four modernizations (industry, agriculture, national defense, and science and technology) by 2000; in the 1990s, again, China's bid to be a WTO member has won Japan's support. In general, although they once appeared critical about China, domestic forces remain strongly against a Japanese containment policy toward China.

China

Various domestic factors in China also cast influence on Beijing's Japan policy. Despite the general consensus and central control of Japan policy, Chinese college students, the public, the military, and even the top leadership still create a changeable environment for Beijing's Japan policy-making.

In 1985, Chinese college students launched a nation-wide boycott of Japanese goods that implicitly opposed Beijing's close economic tie with Japan. In a 1996 best-seller, *China that Can Say No* (Song et al. 1996), a critique of the United States, the young authors pinpointed Japan as a potential enemy in the future. In Chinese political history, students have been a pioneering force of national movement that may support the central government or lead to the fall of a particular leadership. Beijing always tries to use the student activities to its own advantage. Despite shared feeling with the youth, Chinese officials took a cautious and balanced approach toward Japan.

The Chinese public, including students and other social groups, constitutes a wide basis of support for or challenge to China's Japan policy. On the one hand, the public feels superior to Japan, in the sense of culture and history; on the other, it highly respects modern Japanese economic and technological advancements. A 1996 poll indicates that only half of the urban public in three major Chinese cities believe that their country will become the world's strongest economy in the twenty-first century (the United States was seen as first, Japan as second). But the public sees Japan as the top economic rival and half of them see it as a rising or potential military power (*Opinion Analysis,* Oct. 9, 1996: 1–2).

In August 1997, when Chief Cabinet Secretary Kajiyama made his remarks about covering Taiwan in the new Japan-U.S. Defense Cooperation Guidelines, China's major newspapers received a flood of letters urging that media criticize and protest against Japan. This Chinese public reaction was also heard in the military (Internet FBIS-EAS, Sept. 11, 1997).

Before the release of the guidelines, the PLA deputy chief of general staff Xiong Guangkai called the U.S.-Japan guidelines review a result of "Cold War thinking." Xiong especially disagreed with the new guidelines under which Japan's SDF would cooperate with U.S. forces in "areas surrounding Japan" (Internet FBIS-EAS, June 10, 1997).

In foreign policy making, the PLA does not intend to align with any foreign power, including Japan, but does not attempt a harsh Japan policy either. PLA officers believe that Japan has not constituted a military threat to China, and will not until at least 2010. They suggest that China's Japan policy will not change its economic focus, despite Japan's noteworthy military potential. In general, the PLA does not have predominant influence on the Japan-policy decision making. But military intelligence provides valuable information to top Chinese leaders and plays a direct role in that regard (M. Zhang's interviews with two Chinese senior colonels, July 25, 1996).

Among the leadership, some intend to play the Japan card against the United States. A think tank led by Chen Yuan, vice governor of the People's Bank of China and the son of Chen Yun, a powerful late conservative leader, once proposed that China should explore the conflicts between Japan and the United States. He Xin, an analyst at the Chinese Academy of Social Sciences, was a strong advocate of a "quasi-alliance" with Japan. Although this position was not taken as a formal policy and was even criticized by President Jiang Zemin, the idea has been an important strategic alternative (Wilson 1995: 99; interviews by M. Zhang, July 24, 1996).

After the release of the U.S.-Japan Defense Cooperation Guidelines, top Chinese leaders appeared to react differently. Premier Li Peng paid more attention to "the overall good Sino-Japanese relations today," whereas Foreign Minister Qian Qichen complained about the lack of trust between China and Japan and attacked the guidelines for their questionable meaning on Taiwan (Internet FBIS-EAS, Sept. 30, 1997). It was reported that Chinese officials in foreign affairs may fall into "pro-U.S." and "pro-Japan" factions: Liu Huaqiu and Li Zhaoxing belong to the former, and Tang Jiaxuan belongs to the latter (*Chung Yang Jih Pao,* Aug. 1, 1997: 2). Beijing's mainstream foreign policy, however, opposes any political or military alignment, much less an alliance with Japan.

In the near future, Beijing will continue to seek a stable tie with Japan. There would be no fundamental policy shift despite periodic ups and downs. Domestic public factors will not make a Japan policy, but may well be used by the central leadership. In October 1997, for instance, 100 Chinese youths visited Japan for 10 days as part of exchange program commemorating the twenty-fifth anniversary of the normalization of bilateral diplomatic relations (Internet FBIS-EAS, Oct. 16, 1997).

THE BALANCE OF POWER

The situation that "Chinese-Japanese security relations have never been purely bilateral but aspects of larger patterns and developments" has shifted in the 1990s; China and Japan have interacted more directly in an increasingly bilateral context despite the existence of the U.S.-Japan alliance.

First of all, Japan's military power has grown to the extent that both Japan and China have begun to ponder how the power difference between the two military forces would affect their respective and regional security. A "normally" developed Japanese military would also make the Sino-Japanese-U.S. triangle more active.

Table 4.4 contains official Chinese statistics that are widely regarded as being much lower than the real expenditure. Being aware of the ongoing debate on the complicated issue of China's defense budget, we intend not to focus on this topic (Montaperto and Eikenberry 1996). Nevertheless, it is generally accepted that Japan has a much larger GNP (US$4,592 billion in 1994) than China (US$509 billion in 1994) (*Military Balance 1995–1996*); China insisted that its defense expenditure (US$6.4 billion) was only 13.9 percent of Japan's in 1994 (*Renmin Ribao*, Nov. 17, 1995: 3). In 1995, China's defense expenditure was US$7.5 billion compared to Japan's US$50 billion (*Renmin Ribao*, July 3, 1996: 6); in 1996, China's was US$10 billion compared to Japan's US$47 billion. Despite some doubt about China's claims, it is clear that one percent of Japan's GNP defense budget is one of the largest three (together with United States and

---

TABLE 4.3

Japanese Military Expenditure as Percentage of GNP

Items	1991	1992	1993	1994	1995
Defense Share of GNP	1.0	1.0	1.0	1.0	1.0

Source: U.S. Arms Control and Disarmament Agency (ACDA), *World Military Expenditure and Arms Transfers 1995* (Washington, D.C.: ACDA, 1996): 80.

TABLE 4.4

Chinese Military Expenditure as Percentage of GDP

Items	1990	1991	1992	1993	1994	1995
Defense Share of GDP	1.6	1.6	1.6	1.4	1.5	1.4

Source: International Institute for Strategic Studies (IISS), The Military Balance 1995-1996 (London: Oxford University Press): 271.

Russia) due to its long-soaring GNP (*Economist*-Japan Survey, July 13, 1996: 8).

If we put aside the above figures and concentrate on the quality of military forces of the two countries, Japan also seems to be confident about its power status. In December 1995, Japan issued the *National Defense Program Outline in and after FY 1996 (NDPO)*. The *NDPO* stressed "quality over quantity," highlighting a smaller SDF linked to the U.S. forces through their security alliance. The *NDPO* called for a series of downsizings: a 10–20 percent reduction of the current 180,000 army membership, 300 tanks from its total 1,200 tanks, and 100 out of 1,000 major artillery pieces. The navy would retire 10 of 60 major surface combatants while maintaining 16 submarines. The air force would reduce 30 of the current 430 aircraft (Karniol 1996: 52; Internet MOFA *NDPO,* Part IV). While scaling down the quantity of the SDF, the *NDPO* stated that Japan would make qualitative improvements to effectively respond to a variety of situations beyond the defense of Japan (Internet MOFA, *NDPO,* Part III).

Japan, in some military dimensions, has not qualified as a full major power. Japan's air force lacks aerial-refueling capability which is a requisite for power projection; the navy has no aircraft carrier; and the army is short of strategic mobility. Nevertheless, in defense and potential offense, Japan possesses a network of ground and airborne early-warning radars. By 2000, Japan could commission an aircraft carrier battle group armed with existing carrier-compatible F-15s. The navy, while not currently a blue-water force, could be easily transformed for power-projection operation. Four amphibious ships under construction are capable of carrying tanks and personnel. Or, Japan can purchase such ships on a short notice. Japan's new landing ship, the *Osumi,* began sea trials in early 1998. Despite the stated role as a transport ship, it has perhaps the innate capability to conduct sustained helicopter operations, for amphibious assault, and even

TABLE 4.5

Japan's Military Forces, 1996 to 2000

Classification	1996	2000
Ground Force	160,000	Apx. 172,000
Battle tanks	Apx. 900	Apx. 1,050
Main artilleries	Apx. 900	Apx. 900
Maritime Force		
Destroyers	Apx. 50	54
Submarines	16	16
Combat aircraft	Apx. 170	Apx. 170
Air Force		
Combat aircraft	Apx. 400	Apx. 390
Fighters (including combat aircraft)	Apx. 300	Apx. 290

Source: JDA, Defense of Japan 1996, (Tokyo: JDA, 1996): 111.

as a small aircraft carrier. And finally, Japan has joined the United States in producing the most advanced FS-X (F-2) fighters for the coming century. Japanese pilots are well trained for strike aircraft despite the current absence of such aircraft (Cloughley 1996; Bristow 1998).

Despite being a non-nuclear weapons country, Japan has great potential to be such a power. Data published by the Japanese Science and Technology Agency demonstrated that Japan's domestic and overseas plutonium stockpile amounted to about 4.5 tons in the early 1990s and may add up to 100 tons by 2010 (Liao and Sang 1995). Japan also has pursued a Theater Missile Defense (TMD) system. Officials in JDA suggested that Japan would take a five-pronged approach to the TMD that includes detection, identification, target tracking, selection of weapons to employ, and the final interception or destruction of the attacking missiles. Tokyo has not decided to develop and deploy a TMD system. If implemented, such a system could cause a response from China's existing missile strategy (*Defense News,* Apr. 22–28, 1996: 12). In short, Japan possesses quality and potential advantage over the Chinese military.

For now, at least, the PLA enjoys a strategic upper hand over Japan. China is a major nuclear power whose final but successful tests in 1996 were a strong reminder of its nuclear deterrence. An important aspect of the PLA's modernization has been the deployment of ICBMs, with improved range, accuracy, survivability, and penetration against missile defense. DF-31 has a range of 8,000 kilometers; its submarine-launched equivalent, JL-2, has the same range; and DF-41 has a range of 12,000 kilometers. Each of the ICBM systems is capable of delivering 500–700kg warheads (Porteous 1996). But it is known that China lacks early-warning systems, aircraft-carriers, a sufficient number of advanced aircraft, and blue-water fleets. China has 2.5 million strong military personnel and the world's largest army, navy, and air force in number of weapons, and therefore it has a quantitative surplus over Japan. This quantity, however, does not necessarily reflect the quality of the forces (also see chap 2).

China continues to focus on developing a high-technology military. A *Jiefangjun Bao* (Liberation Army Daily) article stressed developing reconnaissance equipment, a remote sensing system, and a battle field information network (Mar. 19, 1996: 6). Another article unveiled scientific research results by the Second Artillery Corps in developing a "large-scale simulated comprehensive strategic missile training system" (*Jiefangjun Bao,* May 16, 1996: 1). Special troops in the ground force exceeded 70 percent of the total army; pilots capable of flying at any time and in all weather conditions constituted 74 percent of the air force. In March 1996, the Nanjing Warring Zone successfully organized a land-sea-air combined military maneuver in the Taiwan Strait. The forces used high-tech equipment and weapons to cross the sea, land on an island, and launch an attack on a mountainous region (*Beijing Review,* July 29–Aug. 4, 1996: 11).

The comparison of the Chinese and Japanese forces provides us further information about the bilateral relationship but leads to no conclusion about the nature and the future of the relationship. We now turn to study how perceptions and domestic factors together with military power have determined the course of their security relations.

SINO-JAPANESE INTERACTION

Sino-Japanese interaction has been characterized by at least two security issues in the 1990s: the Taiwan issue and China's nuclear tests (for the question of U.S.-Japan alliance and China-Japan territorial disputes, see chapter 5). The following section will analyze the bilateral relationship and the dynamics for its development. As we see, the relationship not only has been direct in the military sense but also tends to be more complex.

The Taiwan issue has been a thorn in the Sino-Japanese relationship and turned even more acute in the 1990s. Before the 1994 Asian Games in Hiroshima, Beijing warned Tokyo not to allow top leaders from Taiwan to attend this event. A visit by Taiwan's leader would harm the Sino-Japanese tie because it would violate the One China policy (*Renmin Ribao*, overseas, Sept. 16, 1994: 6). After Japan issued a visa to Taiwan's vice premier Hsu Li-teh, China filed a strong protest (*Renmin Ribao*, overseas, Sept. 23, 1994: 1). Because of this issue, China implied that Japan would not be able to achieve permanent membership in the UN Security Council (*Far Eastern Economic Review*, Oct. 13, 1994: 51).

The Sino-Japanese relationship did not seem to be bogged down in the Taiwan issue. By late 1994 and early 1995, the two countries were exploring a closer military security relationship. While noting the increase of the Chinese military budget, the JDA's 1994 White Paper was positive that China's top priority was economic growth and its military modernization would proceed gradually. In February 1995, General Tetsuya Nishimoto, chairman of the Joint Staff Council, visited China and met General Zhang Wannian, Chief of the General Staff of the People's Liberation Army. This was the first senior uniformed officer of the JDA to visit China (FBIS-EAS, Feb. 21, 1995: 16–17). In early May 1995, Prime Minister Murayama visited Beijing and apologized for Japan's war crimes. The Murayama visit aimed to alleviate the tension between the two countries.

A few days later, however, the Sino-Japanese relationship soured again. This time, China successfully prevented any senior Taiwanese leader from attending the November Asia-Pacific Economic Cooperation (APEC) in Japan. But the new tension emerged over China's nuclear tests. On May 15, China conducted an underground nuclear test and rejected Japan's request to stop future tests. Japan, in turn, sought to halve grant-in-aid to China (FBIS-CHI, June 27, 1995: 13–14). When China ignited another nuclear test in August, Japan issued a sharper protest and threatened to cut a portion of Japan's total aid to China (FBIS-Trends, Aug. 30, 1995: 26). On August 29, Japan took its strongest action by announcing to freeze grants-in-aid to China (FBIS-Trends, Sept. 6, 1995: 9). Although the overall relationship was not decisively affected, this was the first actual open confrontation over a security issue between the two governments after the end of the Cold War. In January 1996, when Japan extended an invitation for Defense Minister Chi Haotian to visit Tokyo, China appeared lukewarm (FBIS-CHI, Jan. 19, 1996: 5).

In short, by the late 1990s, all potential problems and disputes have fully emerged and been exposed in Sino-Japanese relations. China has always been alert about Japanese militarism, and this concern was highlighted when Jiang Zemin visited Seoul in November 1995. Shortly after the U.S. dispatch of aircraft carriers near the Taiwan Strait area, China openly criticized the April 1996 Clinton-Hashimoto summit that confirmed the U.S.-Japan security alliance (*China Daily,* May 23, 1996: 4; *Beijing Review,* May 6–12, 1996: 8–9). The disputes over the Senkaku (Diaoyu) islands and the Law of Sea were also heated up when Japan reclaimed its sovereignty over the Senkaku islands (FBIS-EAS, May 10, 1996: 12). Related to nuclear tests, Japan urged China to increase its military transparency (Internet MOFA, Sept. 1995). In May 1997, Japanese nationalist legislators again landed the disputed Senkaku (Diaoyu) islands and provoked a grave protest from China (*Wen Wei Po,* May 13, 1997: 14). Later on, Chinese activists from Taiwan and Hong Kong sailed to the islands, which resulted in potential military confrontation between China and Japan (see chapter 5).

Meanwhile, the much exposed and shaken relationship did not show any sign of breakup. In April 1996, Chinese foreign minister Qian Qichen visited Japan for four days and met his counterpart Yukihiko Ikeda. *Beijing Review* called the talk "fruitful" (Apr. 15–21, 1996: 4). When China withdrew its demand for allowing so-called peaceful nuclear explosions in the Comprehensive Test Ban Treaty (CTBT) in early June, Ikeda praised China for moving closer to Japan on nuclear issues (FBIS-EAS, June 7, 1996: 11). In the summer, Chinese leaders received several Japanese political party delegations and tried to maintain a healthy development of the bilateral relationship. For his part, Prime Minister Hashimoto repeated Japan's support of China's early accession to the WTO (FBIS-EAS, July 23, 1996: 15). In August, Japan's vice defense chief Naoaki Murata began a series of talks with Chinese military officials, aimed at confidence building and security cooperation. This was the highest military contact between the two countries since 1987 (FBIS-EAS, Aug. 21, 1996: 12). Later, Japan's foreign minister Ikeda called Japan-China relations as important as Japan-U.S. relations (Internet FBIS-EAS, Nov. 12, 1996).

In March 1997, a Japan-China security consultation was held in Tokyo at which the two sides exchanged views on Japan's military role and the new scope of the U.S.-Japan alliance (*Renmin Ribao,* Mar. 17, 1997: 6). In August, JDA announced that Japan would increase the number of military attaches at its embassy in Beijing due to China's increased military significance following the July 1 reversion of Hong Kong to China (Internet FBIS-EAS, Aug. 13, 1997). As part of its plan to strengthen defense exchanges with China, JDA started its coordination with the Chinese government on setting up division-chief-level regular task forces on both sides to discuss defense issues (Internet FBIS-EAS, Aug. 19, 1997). In September, Prime Minister Hashimoto visited Beijing and met top Chinese leaders. Hashimoto took the occasion to announce a loan package, the 202.9 billion yen credit line, to China. Hashimoto and Chinese premier Li Peng agreed to promote high-level exchanges on bilateral defense ties, including visits by uniformed military officers (Internet FBIS-CHI, Sept. 8, 1997). In November, Li Peng paid a six-day official visit to Japan. Li and Hashimoto discussed questions such as Taiwan and Japan-U.S. security alliance. While it supported the idea of One China, Japan stressed the importance of the U.S. military presence in East Asia (Internet FBIS-EAS, Nov. 12, 1997).

In February 1998, Chinese defense minister Chi Haotian visited Japan. Whereas Chi urged Japan to clarify U.S.-Japan alliance's stance on Taiwan, JDA director general Fumio Kyuma invited China for a multilateral security dialogue. The two sides agreed to step up bilateral military exchange of visits by their defense officials. Chi toured several Japanese military facilities, including naval and air bases (Internet FBIS-EAS, Feb. 6, 9, 1998). Chi was the first Chinese defense minister to formally visit Japan in 14 years. In April, Chinese vice president Hu Jingtao visited Japan and encouraged both sides to foster long-term, stable, good-neighborly ties into the twenty-first century. He told the Japanese that Jiang Zemin would visit Japan in autumn as the first Chinese president in history (Internet China Daily, Apr. 24, 1998). In May, JDA director general Fumio Kyuma visited China. In order to "build future-oriented Japan-China relations," Hiromu Nonaka, acting secretary-general of the LDP, arranged a Japanese delegation to visit the Nanjing Massacre Memorial (Internet South China Morning Post, May 8, 1998).

In general, the two countries have not truly resolved any serious problems, and this has left the two governments in a face-to-face situation. The relationship could move to a further decline and eventual confrontation. Or, as it appears now, the relationship could become more transparent and under better control.

Undoubtedly, the deterioration of Sino-Japanese relations in the 1990s is first of all related to the military growth in both countries. The "distribution of power" between the two countries has transformed rapidly and appears to have triggered the mutual sense of threat and a downturn in the relationship. "Power" alone, however, does not seem to explain the changing Sino-Japanese relations. Domestic influence and perceptions play a significant role.

Like many scholars, Chinese leaders paid little attention to Japan's demands for stopping nuclear tests. But since 1994, the Japanese government has come under increasing domestic pressure to take firmer actions against Beijing. Major political parties have called for deeper cuts in aid to China, and the media have criticized the Japanese administration for failing to deal more forcefully with China. On August 17, 1995, for example, Japan's three largest parties (the LDP, the New Frontier Party, and the SDP) issued sharply worded protests over China's nuclear test and called for more cuts in Japanese aid to China. Under this unusual pressure, Foreign Minister Yohei Kono personally summoned Chinese ambassador to Japan Xu Dunxin to the MOFA and protested the Chinese action. At the same time, Japan decided to cut an unspecified amount of grants-in-aid to China.

Japan's decision was also pressed by the media. *Nihon Keizai Shimbun* commented that the Japanese government lost face when Beijing ignored its protests. *Mainichi Shimbun* criticized Prime Minister Murayama's failure to react more promptly (FBIS-Trends, Aug. 30, 1995: 26–28).

Finally, on August 29, Japan decided to freeze grants-in-aid to China except a small portion of humanitarian assistance, the strongest step in recent years to protest China's nuclear testing program (FBIS-Trends, Sept. 6, 1995: 9).

Coupled with domestic influence, individual perceptions played a decisive role in making both countries' policy. There are numerous Chinese authors who suspect Japan's naval strategy and buildup is expansionist and potentially dangerous (*Conmilit,* July 1991, Nov. 1993, Mar. 1995). In an article discussing surface-to-surface missiles, an author wrote that "once it is required to do so, Japan would soon have ICBMs; economic power and technological capacity also firmly set Japan at the verge of possessing nuclear missiles" (Z. Zheng 1996). The Chinese official newspaper *Renmin Ribao* routinely warned against the rise of Japanese militarism from a historical and contemporary perspective (Aug. 8, 1995: 7; Aug. 16, 1995: 7; Aug. 31, 1995: 9; July 3, 1996: 6). For Japan's part, the JDA's 1996 White Paper, for the first time in two decades, included China in its annual assessment of potential threats by citing China's military buildup and military exercises over Taiwan.

SUMMARY

In sum, prompted by military growth in both Japan and China, mutual suspicion increased and domestic politics tended to press on both governments. But military growth alone did not result in the complicated Sino-Japanese tie, no matter how "power" is defined. The relationship has deteriorated partially because of changing perceptions and domestic dynamics. Overall, however, neither country's leaders have gone so far as to treat the other's as a threat. Economic interests and domestic politics also have constrained a hostile policy. In the near future, military power in both countries will continue to grow; the distribution of power, together with changing perceptions and domestic factors, will determine how the two countries react to each other.

In that regard, as demonstrated in this chapter, the United States will shape the Sino-Japanese relationship to a considerable extent. The bottom line is that the United States is the superpower in the triad and can make the Sino-Japanese relationship tense, stable, or unpredictable. In other words, either American presence or absence in East Asia will make a difference for the two Asian nations.

5

The Triad as Reciprocal Relations: How Does It Work?

In chapter 2 through chapter 4, we have analyzed the nature of the Sino-Japanese-U.S. strategic triangle by investigating their bilateral relations. The results indicate that the three countries have been entangled in various issues and disputes and the relationship generally is one of great uncertainty. By no means, however, can this relationship be characterized as hostile. All three countries have made efforts to move the relationship in a stable and mutually beneficial direction.

The bilateral studies, however, have left a key question unanswered: does the triad exist? If it does, how do we describe the behavioral pattern of this triad?

In this chapter, we examine the hypothesis of reciprocation in the Sino-Japanese-U.S. triad by observing the pattern of behavioral interaction. First of all, in order to verify whether the triad exists, we study *how one actor affects the interaction between the other two actors in the triad* through consecutive and seemingly related events. We then analyze whether each country's behavior in later events reciprocates their counterparts' prior behaviors. As a result, we take an inductive approach in this chapter and hope to provide more evidence on the triadic behavioral pattern. Differing from the realist two-against-one alignment studies, our focus is reciprocation.

Before we proceed, some words are necessary on how to examine whether a reaction by a country (or countries) in a later event reciprocates an action by another country (or countries). For such a purpose, we need to verify the direct link between the action and reaction, which can be a policy statement, a planned occurrence, or any cause-effect evidence. Common sense tells us, however, that any reaction may be caused by many factors instead of a single event or previous action. Thus, the three cases aside, we also briefly address other elements, events, and countries that may have impact on a country's reciprocal behavior. Nevertheless, if other elements appear to predominate or negate the direct link we found between the three cases, no relationship—or only a weak—one exists amongst the three cases we chose for this study; in that case, we cannot confirm the assumption of trilateral reciprocity for the U.S.-Chinese-Japanese relationship.

In any event, the Sino-Japanese-U.S. triad is a relatively new configuration. During the Cold War era (1945–1990), Japan as a U.S. ally hardly played an autonomous role or interacted directly with China in security dimensions. The end of the Cold War clearly marked a new era of Japan's increasingly independent military functions. Even at the end of the twentieth century, however, the triadic image has not fully emerged. This reality confines this book to certain methods and evidence on the strategic triangle. As a result, we focus on a series of events in 1996 that at least partially demonstrate the existence and the behavioral pattern of the triad. These events are the Taiwan crisis in March, the U.S.-Japan summit in April, and the Sino-Japanese Diaoyu/Senkaku island dispute in September-October. As a method in the each case study, we analyze how Country A affects the bilateral relationship between Country B and Country C. If each country affects the bilateral interaction of the other two, we confirm the existence of the triangle. We then examine whether the three countries reciprocate other's action and reaction. The evidence would explain at least one type of behavior within the triad.

THE TAIWAN CRISIS (MARCH 1996)

In this section, we first discuss how China and the United States interacted with each other during the Taiwan crisis. We then analyze whether Japan affected the Sino-U.S. interaction.

In retrospect, the Taiwan crisis was precipitated by many historical and ongoing events. But the People's Liberation Army (PLA)'s massive and condensed military exercises in March 1996 clearly dramatized Sino-U.S. relations. Through the exercises, China attempted to threaten pro-independence elements before Taiwan's general election on March 23.

On March 6, Beijing announced that the PLA would conduct missile-launching exercises in the East China Sea and the South China Sea from March 8 to March 15. The targets were about 30 miles off Taiwan's port cities of Jilong and Gaoxiong, respectively (*Renmin Ribao,* Mar. 6, 1996: 1). Shortly after the announcement, the U.S. Congress' House leadership signed a non-binding resolution calling for U.S. forces to be sent into battle if China attacked Taiwan, while the White House remained cautious and warned both China and Taiwan not to be provocative (*Washington Times,* Mar. 6, 1996: A18). On March 8, China launched two (later sources reported three; see *Washington Post,* Mar. 12, 1996: A10) M-9 missiles carrying dummy warheads that landed inside the target areas. U.S. military leaders denounced the exercises; the aircraft carrier *USS Independence* was then near Taiwan and the guided-missile cruiser *USS Bunker Hill* was close enough to monitor the missile flights (*New York Times,* Mar. 8, 1996: A1; *Philadelphia Inquirer,* Mar. 9, 1996: 10). On March 13, the PLA fired a fourth missile into waters west of Gaoxiong (*Washington Post,* Mar. 14, 1996: A22). On March 16, Beijing announced that the PLA Second Artillery had successfully fired four surface-to-surface missiles and accomplished exercise tasks (*Renmin Ribao,* Mar. 16, 1996: 1).

On March 10, when the aforementioned missile exercises were still going on, Beijing announced that the PLA would conduct live-ammunition naval and air force maneuvers in the South China Sea and the East China Sea from March 12 to 20. The exercise zone was off China's Guangdong and Fujian provinces and near the Taiwan-controlled Jinmen and Penghu islands (*Renmin Ribao,* Mar. 10, 1996: 1).

Secretary of State Warren Christopher accused China of the "reckless" military provocations against Taiwan. President Bill Clinton and other top policymakers directed the aircraft carrier *Independence* to move closer toward the Taiwan Strait and decided to send another aircraft carrier *Nimitz* to the Taiwan Strait. At the same time, however, the U.S. government maintained the doctrine of "strategic ambiguity" by not clarifying how it would react to a Chinese invasion of Taiwan (*Los Angeles Times,* Mar. 11, 1996: 1; *Washington Post,* Mar. 12, 1996: A10).

China charged that the Clinton administration and Taiwan's leaders had touched off a crisis, and Foreign Minister Qian Qichen warned at a news conference that "Taiwan is a part of China's territory and is not a protectorate of the United States" (*New York Times,* Mar. 12, 1996: A6). On March 12, the PLA's warships and fighter aircraft began live-fire military exercises, practicing bombing runs and drills (*Washington Post,* Mar. 13, 1996: A18). At the same time, China sent an unambiguous signal to the United States that it did not intend to invade or attack Taiwan. For their part, U.S. officials expressed their belief that there would be no direct military confrontation between the two sides of Chinese (*New York Times,* Mar. 13, 1996: A3). By March 13, China had fired four dummy warhead missiles into waters near Gaoxiong and Jilong, and Chinese rear admiral Gao Yuanfa said that the Chinese navy would repel any U.S. incursion into its territorial waters (See *Washington Post,* Mar. 14, 1996: A22).

As the crisis continued, the U.S. Congress House International Relations Committee passed a resolution to defend Taiwan against invasion, missile attack, or blockade. But the administration insisted that there would be no immediate threat to Taiwan in the near future. Assistant Secretary of State Winston Lord testified before the House that the administration would not support a bill that could complicate the current situation (*Washington Times,* Mar. 15, 1996: A1; *Washington Post,* Mar. 15, 1996: A24).

The crisis continued on March 16 when Beijing announced that the PLA would conduct joint live-ammunition land, sea, and air exercises in the Taiwan Strait from March 18 to March 25. The declared zone is off Fujian Province and near the Taiwan-controlled outlying islands Mazu and Wuchiu (*Renmin Ribao,* Mar. 16, 1996: 1). At the time, the U.S. aircraft carrier *Nimitz* continued to move toward the Pacific Ocean from the Middle East but never entered the Taiwan Strait. The United States negotiated with Taiwan on arms sales and agreed to sell Stinger surface-to-air missiles to Taiwan (*United Daily News,* Mar. 20, 21, 1996: 1). The PLA's exercises, including advanced aircraft, warships, missiles, and electronic equipment, actually ended on March 20, three days before Taiwan's election (*Renmin Ribao,* Mar. 21, 1996: 1). At this point, the weeks-long crisis started to cool down.

China's military exercises worried many Asian nations, but foremost Japan. Japan's reaction to the U.S.-China confrontation had clearly favored the U.S. side. Nevertheless, after the case is fully examined, we will see that Tokyo might have helped the Beijing-Washington tie in a positive direction. Although Beijing and Washington mainly determined the result of the Taiwan crisis, that did not necessarily exclude an impact by a third party. In general, Japan took a very restrained position, both in its support of the United States and in its opposition to China.

On March 6, the day China announced its missile exercises, Japanese Foreign Ministry expressed its opinion that heightening tensions over the Taiwan Strait was not conducive for peace and stability in East Asia. Japan was concerned that sea traffic near the test area might be affected by the missile tests. The Japanese government urged both sides of the Chinese to solve their conflict peacefully (FBIS-EAS, Mar. 6, 1996: 13). The Japanese-U.S. coordination on the Taiwan crisis was also visible at the time. It was reported that the United States would brief Japan on Chinese (and Russian and North Korean) strategic nuclear missiles under a bilateral pact signed a month earlier. According to the pact, the United States would provide Japan with information from U.S. spy satellites and intelligence agencies, and for the first time Japan would receive comprehensive data on strategic missiles (FBIS-EAS, Mar. 11, 1996: 20).

After China started its live-fire naval–air force joint exercises, the Japanese Foreign Ministry voiced concerns that the exercises were near Japanese territorial waters and only 60 kilometers away from its island of Yonaguni (FBIS-EAS, Mar. 12, 1996: 16). The Japanese government stated further its belief that the United States played a very important role in maintaining peace and stability in the Asia-Pacific region. At the time, the U.S. aircraft carrier *Independence* was dispatched from a military base in Japan to monitor Chinese drills (FBIS-EAS, Mar. 13, 1996: 12). In addition to its own surveillance, Japan asked the U.S. government for information on the ongoing situation over the Taiwan Strait (FBIS-EAS, Mar. 13, 1996: 9).

Nevertheless, Japan did not clarify whether it would fulfill its alliance obligations with the United States to fight China should a war occur over the Taiwan Strait. Rather, Japan's criticism of China did not go so far as to downgrade their bilateral relationship.

Responding to some LDP members' requests to postpone a visit by Chinese foreign minister Qian Qichen, Prime Minister Ryutaro Hashimoto argued that the visit would be a "good opportunity" to indicate the Japanese desire for Chinese restraint and to show Japan's concern over the Taiwan Strait situation (FBIS-EAS, Mar. 13, 1996: 6). According to Japanese Foreign Ministry spokesman Hiroshi Hashimoto, the Japanese government did not foresee imminent military conflict in the region. The spokesman even suggested that "China, in principle, has a right to carry out military exercises using the high seas, so long as those exercises will not hinder the usage of international seas by other countries. Up until now, we cannot consider that these present exercises violate international law." The "situation is under control," and the Japanese Self-Defense Forces were not on alert (FBIS-EAS, Mar. 13, 1996: 8–9).

Undoubtedly, Japan would side with the United States in any situation concerning a Sino-U.S. conflict over Taiwan. But it seemed that Japan's commitment and involvement also could be limited. To quote the spokesman again:

> [T]he United States is our ally. We fully trust the United States. We fully understand that the United States is determined to continue to play an important role for peace and stability in the region. . . . China is a very important neighbor for us, and we just hope that the Chinese Government will understand the concerns expressed by the Japanese Government (FBIS-EAS, Mar. 13, 1996: 10).

It is clear from the spokesman that Japan would limit its involvement in a potential U.S.-Chinese conflict over Taiwan. To be more specific, the spokesman stated that "I did not say that our position is different from that of the United States, or that we disagree with the United States. However, our position is much more vulnerable than that of the United States, so that what we can do and say is very limited" (FBIS-EAS, Mar. 13, 1996: 11). Prime Minister Hashimoto even hoped "the United States will exercise self-control" (FBIS-EAS, Mar. 15, 1996: 4). This kind of opinion was also shared by some influential former officials. When asked about what Japan could do if the PLA attacked Taiwan, a former director general of the Japan Defense Agency said that that "has nothing to do with Japan's security and peace, it would be difficult for Japan to take action" (FBIS-EAS, Apr. 19, 1996: 14).

As discussed earlier, the United States and China had communicated over the danger of a military clash. Japan prevented a deepened Sino-U.S. tension in this regard. This assessment can be confirmed from the Japanese statements we have cited and the following U.S. and Chinese responses to Japan's concerns.

American ambassador to Japan Walter Mondale briefed Japanese leaders that the United States sent the aircraft carriers *Independence* and *Nimitz* near Taiwan because the Chinese military pressure would escalate if left ignored. But Mondale added that Washington had no intention of imposing an economic blockade against China, a scenario that had worried Japan (FBIS-EAS, Mar. 14, 1996: 1). If the United States did not even attempt an economic sanction, we also can assume that it did not want a military conflict with China. The United States considered Japan to be an important factor in its military action.

As for China, when asked for comments on the dispatch of the US *Independence* from a Japanese naval base, Foreign Minister Qian simply warned that "the Taiwan issue is the internal affair of China, the foreign forces should not make irresponsible remarks or take action regarding China's internal affair" (*Beijing Review,* Mar. 25–31, 1996: 8). Chinese spokesman Shen Guofang warned Tokyo not to withhold promised low-interest yen loans because of China's drills (FBIS-CHI, Mar. 19, 1996: 1). Our survey of China's reactions toward Japan during March 1996 found only a few statements and no diplomatic action against Japan. It shows that Beijing did not worry about a joint U.S.-Japanese fight against China during the Taiwan crisis. This is clearly a result of Japan's restrained attitude and action.

Thus, Japan, China, and the United States did interact with each other within a triadic framework. Although Japan's restrained behavior only affected Sino-U.S. relations to a limited extent, the interaction demonstrated partial evidence of the functioning of the strategic triad.

THE CLINTON-HASHIMOTO SUMMIT (APRIL 1996)

In this section, we study the U.S.-Japanese summit in April and examine how China might have influenced the summit resolutions. This case offers further evidence of the existence of the U.S.-Japanese-Chinese strategic triangle.

President Bill Clinton arrived at Tokyo's Haneda Airport on April 16 for a three-day state visit to Japan and held talks with Prime Minister Hashimoto. Japanese foreign minister Yukihiko Ikeda told a news conference that the summit "will be very significant in that it is intended to forge a new Japan-U.S. partnership for the future" (FBIS-EAS, Apr. 16, 1996: 2).

The two leaders signed two documents. One was a message to the people of Japan and the United States. The other was the Joint Japan-U.S. Security Declaration. The latter is of particular significance for the U.S.-Japan-China strategic triangle. In it, the two leaders stated:

> We are witnessing the emergence of an Asia-Pacific community. The Asia-Pacific region has become the most dynamic area of the globe.
>
> The U.S.-Japan security relationship, based on the Treaty of Mutual Cooperation and Security between the United States and Japan, remains the cornerstone for achieving common security objectives, and for maintaining a stable and prosperous environment for the Asia-Pacific region as we enter the twenty-first century.

The President and the Prime Minister welcomed the April 15, 1996 signature of the Agreement between the Government of the United States of America and the Government of Japan Concerning Reciprocal Provision of Logistic Support, Supplies and Services between the Armed Forces of the United States of America and the Self-Defense Forces of Japan.

The two leaders stressed the importance of peaceful resolution of problems in the region. They emphasized that it is extremely important for the stability and prosperity of the region that China play a positive and constructive role, and in this context, stressed the interest of both countries in furthering cooperation with China (FBIS-EAS, Apr. 17, 1996: 13–15).

The Tokyo summit addressed a series of urgent issues such as the rape of a 12–year old Okinawan schoolgirl by U.S. military service men, the U.S. military presence in Japan, deterrence against states like North Korea, TMD, and anti-terrorism (FBIS-EAS, Apr. 18, 1996: 5). From the security declaration and the timing of the summit, however, it is evident that China was a major factor in the U.S.-Japan meeting. China's impact on the Tokyo summit has two aspects. First, China's military exercises near Taiwan caused anxiety and may have prompted a strengthened US-Japan alliance at the summit. Second, China's warning against the summit may have prevented Washington and Tokyo from forming an explicit and permanent anti-China alliance.

At a news conference, Clinton stated that the two leaders "discussed Taiwan and China extensively as well as the recent tension in the Taiwan Strait. It is obvious that our partnership is designed to try to preserve the peace for all peoples in this region" (FBIS-EAS, Apr. 17, 1996: 6). Hashimoto also emphasized the value of a peaceful resolution of the Taiwan question while both leaders reiterated the One China policy. The summit indicated the U.S. and Japanese concerns about China's military action in the Asia-Pacific region. Chinese Foreign Ministry spokesman Shen Guofang also implied that the PLA's military exercises could be an issue for the Tokyo summit by stating that foreign countries should not interfere in China's domestic affairs (FBIS-EAS, Apr. 18, 1996: 15). As we see, China's hostile action over Taiwan somewhat reinforced the U.S.-Japan alliance at the summit. Several years after the end of the Cold War, the United States and Japan had tried to redefine the role and rationale of their alliance. An assertive Chinese military power in 1996 probably well served such an opportunity.

Moreover, the China factor seems to have become a long-term concern within the U.S.-Japan alliance. In June 1997, JDA director general Fumio Kyuma indicated that Japan needs to consider China in future defense: "If Japan-U.S. relations are stable, they would be a deterrent against trouble in the Asia-Pacific region" (Internet FBIS-EAS, July 1, 1997).

Yet the 1996 Tokyo summit did not show strong evidence of a two-against-one scenario. Despite the confirmed U.S.-Japan cooperation on security issues, the two countries did not gird up for a long-term containment policy. We can identify at least one important China factor in this regard: the summit's neutral and even somewhat positive statement on U.S. and Japanese policy toward China, possibly due to Beijing's warnings against a Washington-Tokyo "collusion." Or, put it differently, both Washington and Tokyo had a good assessment of Chinese thinking and did not want to alienate China. They further understand that China could do a lot of harm if an anti-China alliance was formed.

Before and during the Tokyo summit, Beijing warned repeatedly against an anti-China U.S.-Japanese alliance. Visiting Japan in early April, about two weeks before the Clinton-Hashimoto summit, Chinese foreign minister Qian Qichen opposed a strengthened U.S.-Japan alliance because of the tension over the Taiwan Strait. He urged that the bilateral alliance should not go beyond its bilateral arrangement (*Renmin Ribao,* Apr. 4, 1996: 6). After Japan and the United States issued the Security Declaration, Chinese foreign ministry spokesman Shen Guofang also expressed the hope that the U.S.-Japan security treaty "will not exceed the range for mutual defense." According to him, if the Japanese Self-Defense Forces should try to build up its military or expand the range of its defense, it would force various Asian countries to exercise enhanced alertness (FBIS-EAS, Apr. 18, 1996: 6). As we see, the final version of the Tokyo summit documents was carefully worded to evade the impression of containment of China. Prime Minister Hashimoto considered "positive engagement of China in the international community to be important" and supported China's early accession to the World Trade Organization (FBIS-EAS, Apr. 18, 1996: 8). In response to the Clinton-Hashimoto joint declaration's call for cooperation with China, Shen echoed that Beijing intended to strengthen cooperative relations with both the United States and Japan (FBIS-EAS, Apr. 18, 1996: 15–16).

The point is that the countries of the Tokyo summit were not determined to view China as a threat, and later development of triangular relations has not demonstrated a two-against-one trend either. In April 1997, U.S. secretary of defense William Cohen visited Japan and told reporters that China has nothing to fear from the U.S. troop presence: "It is not designated against China at all, but to maintain stability in the region" (*Washington Post,* Apr. 9, 1997: 24). Visiting Washington in the same month, Prime Minister Hashimoto reiterated his positive attitude toward China and expected China to play a constructive role in international security (Internet FBIS-EAS, Apr. 29, 1997). In July, Deputy Assistant Secretary of Defense Kurt Campbell and the deputy chief of mission of the U.S. Embassy in Japan went to Beijing to brief the 1996 summit. In early 1998, top defense officials from the three countries exchanged visits. Of course, the potential for an anti-China trend exists, and, as pointed out by an article in *Beijing Review,* China is "sensitive to any move by the Americans and Japanese to seek a closer alliance" (*Beijing Review,* June 16–22, 1997).

From the interaction among the three countries, China appeared to have influenced the result of the Tokyo summit. The joint documents from the summit clearly bore a Chinese imprint. The phenomenon that one country affects the bilateral relationship of the others is important evidence on the existence of a triad.

THE DIAOYU/SENKAKU DISPUTE
(SEPTEMBER–OCTOBER 1996)

In early September 1996, China and Japan rekindled a sovereignty dispute over the small islands called Diaoyu by the Chinese or Senkaku by the Japanese. This case is applied to understand how the United States affected the Sino-Japanese dispute.

Beijing claims to have exercised sovereignty over the area since the sixteenth century, whereas Tokyo insists that its rights derive from the takeover of Okinawa in 1879 and the formal incorporation of the Senkaku islands after defeating China's naval fleet in 1895. By the end of World War II, the United States had occupied the islands. The Sino-Japanese territorial dispute was further compounded in 1972 by the U.S. decision to turn over the administration of Diaoyu/Senkaku islands to Japan, along with Okinawa. At present, Japan controls the disputed islands. The new dispute assumes added significance because geological studies suggest possible extensive oil and gas deposits in the area.

The dispute also heated up in September because of the anniversary of an important historical event in the same month. On September 18, 1931, Japan invaded Shenyang, a Chinese city in the Northeast, precipitating conflict between the two nations that lasted until the end of World War II. On September 6, 1996, the official English *China Daily*'s commentary warned against the Japanese military buildup, such as its US$50 billion defense expenditure in 1995 and its claims to Diaoyu islands (*China Daily,* Sept. 6, 1996: 4). On September 9, members of the nationalist Japan Youth Federation repaired a lighthouse on the islands to dramatize Tokyo's claim (the group installed the lighthouse in July). The next day, China lodged a formal protest against Tokyo's "connivance" with the Japanese rightists but fell short of noting the possibility of sending military forces to the islands (*South China Morning Post,* Sept. 13, 1996: 8).

In early September, the PLA set up a Diaoyu islands "operational group" for emergency plans and dispatched naval ships near the Diaoyu islands (*Sing Tao Jih Pao,* Sept. 12, 1996: A2). Meanwhile Chinese president Jiang Zemin ordered university officials to prevent students from staging protests over the island issue in mainland China, as demonstrations were on the rise in both Hong Kong and Taiwan. An official circular from Beijing urged Chinese scholars and students to refrain from drastic words and deeds and assured them of the government's capability to safeguard sovereignty (*Hong Kong Standard,* Sept. 17, 1996: 1; *Ming Pao,* Sept. 17, 1996: A4).

On September 13 and 14, PLA units deployed in the Shenyang Military Region conducted a large-scale army-navy-air force combined exercise in landing operations, based on a scenario that a foreign army had occupied a series of islands. On September 18, the Chinese navy also conducted a comprehensive supply exercise in the East China Sea waters, involving a variety of naval vessels and aircraft. China's official Xinhua News Agency reported that the two exercises demonstrated the PLA's combat effectiveness as well as its determination to defend China's territory (*Wen Wei Po,* Sept. 25, 1996: A2). *China Daily* carried a large photo of the supply exercise on its front page (Sept. 25, 1996: 1). (Taiwan conducted missile drills near the Diaoyu islands on September 17, 19, and 23 but denied their link to the island dispute. See Internet FBIS-CHI, Sept. 27, 1996.)

Japanese foreign minister Ikeda sought China's understanding of Japan's position and assured Chinese foreign minister Qian of efforts to calm the dispute over the islands. He promised Qian that Tokyo would not officially recognize the lighthouse built by the right-wing Japanese group (Internet FBIS-EAS, Sept. 26, 1996). But on September 26, the dispute turned deadly when a protester from Hong Kong drowned after jumping into the rough sea in front of a flotilla of Japanese vessels. Chinese foreign ministry spokesman Shen Guofang mourned the death and reiterated China's territorial claim (*Ta Kung Pao,* Sept. 27, 1996: A1). On September 30, the Nanjing Military Region and the East Sea Fleet reportedly sent more than 10 warplanes and naval vessels to cruise past and fly over the Diaoyu islands. Both the Japanese and American military kept watch over the entire military action, without any encounter with the PLA (*Sing Tao Jih Pao,* Oct. 10, 1996: A2).

On October 2, Xu Dunxin, Chinese ambassador to Japan, stressed the significance of Sino-Japanese relations but urged Japan to match words with deeds (Internet FBIS-CHI, Oct. 14, 1996). On October 6, protesters from Taiwan and Hong Kong slipped past Japanese coast guard vessels and landed on one of the disputed islands (Internet CNN, Oct. 6, 1996; *United Daily News,* Oct. 8, 1996: 1). Tokyo and Beijing maintained different positions over the islands. According to the Japanese Foreign Ministry, Tokyo holds the "medium line principle" while Beijing insists on the "natural prolongation principle" for the delimitation of the continental shelf between Japan and China (Internet Japanese Foreign Ministry, Oct. 16, 1996). A *China Daily* article provided what it viewed as historical evidence supporting China's claims to the islands (Oct. 19, 1996: 4).

The Chinese military took a tough approach toward the island dispute. A senior officer commented that there would be no new Li Hongzhang in present China, who, as the representative of the late Qing Dynasty government, ceded Taiwan along with the Diaoyu islands to Japan by signing the Shimonoseki Treaty (*Ming Pao,* Oct. 21, 1996: A6). On October 24, a Japanese government spokesman said that "it is desirable to resolve the dispute peacefully," and Tokyo considered sending a special envoy to Beijing for such a mission (Internet FBIS-EAS, Oct. 25, 1996). On October 29, Chinese vice foreign minister Tang Jiaxuan visited Japan and met his counterpart Shunji Yanai. Both sides agreed to a calm approach on the island dispute (Internet FBIS-EAS, Oct. 30, 1996). But differences remained. In meeting with Prime Minister Hashimoto, Tang asked Japan to remove the lighthouse. Hashimoto asked Tang to understand that there are limits to what the Japanese government can do as a law-governed state (Internet FBIS-EAS, Oct. 31, 1996).

As a result, the two-month-long territorial friction between China and Japan cooled down, yet without any solution. The tension could escalate again and the potential for crisis remains. This time, at least, restraint reined an open confrontation.

The United States could play a very crucial role in the Sino-Japanese quarrel over the Diaoyu/Senkaku islands for various reasons. First, the United States transferred the administration power of the islands to Japan in 1972 and is in the position to explain that legal transformation. Second, as Japan's ally, the United States could become directly involved in any

Sino-Japanese territorial conflict. Should the United States recognize Japanese sovereignty over the Diaoyu/Senkaku islands, it would fulfill security commitments to Japan.

Nevertheless, the United States had responded to the Sino-Japanese dispute by non-action, which had its own rationale and affected Sino-Japanese interaction. In general, Washington did not want to see the security situation in East Asia deteriorate over the territorial dispute.

In response to the U.S. statement that it does not recognize any country's sovereignty over the Diaoyu islands, Chinese Foreign Ministry spokesman Shen Guofang said that the United States should respect China's stand and that there is no need for the United States to comment on this issue. Meanwhile, Shen reiterated Beijing's stand "to lay aside disputes and carry out joint development" with Japan. He reminded people of Japan's militarism in the past and urged both Japan and the United States to make contributions to Asian security (*Ta Kung Pao,* Sept. 13, 1996: A1; Internet FBIS-CHI, Sept. 16, 1996). In any event, the U.S. position on the islands did not provoke China or worsen the existing tension between China and Japan.

According to a report, some Japanese officials expected the United States to be obliged in use of military force to protect the Japanese claims to the disputed islands, citing the Japan-U.S. Security Treaty. But Ambassador Mondale noted that the United States takes no position on who owns the islands and that American forces would not be compelled by the treaty to intervene in a dispute over them (*New York Times,* Sept. 16, 1996: A8). It was reported that on September 30 the PLA sent two missile destroyers and two escort vessels 30 nautical miles off the Diaoyu islands with four J-8 and four Su-27 fighters flying over the ships. Both the U.S. and Japanese forces monitored the operation, but did not take further action (*Sing Tao Jih Pao,* Oct. 10, 1996: A2).

In May 1997, the Diaoyu/Senkaku dispute erupted again as Chinese civilians from Hong Kong, Taiwan, and the United States sailed toward the island. Japan dispatched patrol ships and helicopters to expel the Chinese boats and collided with a boat from Hong Kong. In addition to vocal protests against Japan from both the mainland China and Taiwan, the PLA sent fighters, including SU-27s, near the disputed area (*United Daily News,* May 27, 1997: 1, 3). Again, the United States did not take any action but called for a peaceful solution. Further, a State Department spokesman reiterated that Washington did not support any party's claim over the disputed island and that the United States handed over only the administrative power of the island to Japan, an action that did not involve the issue of sovereignty (*United Daily News,* May 29, 1997: 1).

The U.S. non-action probably made neither China nor Japan happy. For example, a Japanese article in *Jiyu* complained about the U.S. government's "ambiguity" on the Senkaku issue and censured its China policy as "appeasement" (Yamazaki 1997). But any U.S. commitment to either party would have caused serious response from the other. If, for instance, the United States recognized Japan's sovereignty and even took military measures to support Japan, China would have reciprocated violently. American ambiguity and non-action essentially stabilized the Sino-Japanese tension. How the United States affected the bilateral relationship between China and Japan attests to the existence of the strategic triangle.

THE RECIPROCAL BEHAVIOR

The three case studies we have provided constitute an empirical analysis about the existence of the U.S.-Chinese-Japanese strategic triangle. Based upon the three case studies, this section further examines the reciprocal pattern of the triangular behavior, which has both theoretical and policy implications.

In order to understand how China, the United States, and Japan reciprocated during the Taiwan crisis, it is necessary to review what events or behavior might have preceded the crisis. The purpose is to see whether the three countries reciprocated in kind.

China's hostility toward the United States in March 1996 can be traced back to May 1995 when Taiwan's leader Lee Tenghui was granted a visa to visit the United States. China responded immediately by calling off high-level meetings with the United States and conducting a series of military exercises targeted at Taiwan in late 1995 (*Washington Times,* May 27, 1995: A11; *Washington Post,* May 29, 1995: A17; *Washington Post,* July 24, 1995: A1; *Economist,* July 29, 1995: 23).[1] China's *Renmin Ribao* editorial described the U.S. invitation to Lee as "playing with fire" (*Renmin Ribao,* June 11, 1995). By January 1996, Beijing had escalated military action and informed Washington of its plans for military exercises before the March election in Taiwan (*New York Times,* Jan. 24, 1996: A1, A3).

The United States government defended its invitation to Lee as private or unofficial. At the same time, the United States continued to criticize China on human rights, trade, and arms-sales issues. On February 13, 1996, Secretary of Defense William Perry stated at the U.S. National Defense University that the best China policy is constructive engagement but "we are not committed to engagement at any price" (Internet Department of Defense, Feb. 13, 1996). Thus, in March 1996, both China and the United States reciprocated each other's previous hostile behavior.

At the time, Japan also was caught in the crisis. We now turn to see how Japan decided to support the United States but with great restraint.

Japan had its own concerns and interests during the Taiwan crisis. In 1995, Sino-Japanese relations had deteriorated as China continued nuclear weapons testing and military exercises targeted at Taiwan. Owing to Beijing's rejection of its request for halting nuclear testing, Tokyo decided to suspend its grant-in-aid to China in August, the strongest signal it had ever given (FBIS-Trends, Sept. 1995: 9). With regard to China's military exercises, Japan did not wish to see free navigation blocked across the Taiwan Strait. At bottom, both nuclear testing and military exercises by China were seen as threats by Japan. Consequently, these earlier events prompted Japan to side with the United States. This is the first round of negative reciprocal behavior, in which China reciprocated the U.S. hostility in 1995 whereas the United States and Japan reciprocated China's military exercises by sending warships or criticizing China's action.

Based on the Taiwan crisis in March, it is not difficult to understand why China became a major factor in the U.S.-Japan summit in April 1996. Although the Tokyo summit had been scheduled in 1995, the decision to extend U.S.-Japan security cooperation from a Japan-centered mission to an Asia-Pacific regional commitment can be logically linked to what had just happened in the Taiwan Strait. As both Clinton and Hashimoto claimed, they were concerned about the Taiwan Strait situation and wished to see a peaceful instead of violent solution to the Taiwan issue. In this regard, the United States and Japan reciprocated the Chinese exercises in March by strengthening the bilateral alliance. In particular, the ambiguity about Taiwan at the summit was a warning message to China.

We now turn to China's reaction toward the Tokyo summit from the perspective of U.S. and Japanese previous behavior. As discussed earlier, Beijing questioned the purpose of the Tokyo summit. China's anxiety mostly derived from U.S.-Japanese collaboration against the PLA's exercises during the Taiwan crisis. In May, *China Daily* ran an article entitled "US-Japan Pact Does More Harm Than Good," suspecting that the China threat theory was used to justify the consolidation of the U.S.-Japan security system (May 23, 1996: 4). Public opinion in China was also somewhat opposed to the U.S.-Japan alliance (Zhang 1997; *Opinion Analysis* Oct. 9 1996: 2).

Vocal criticism aside, China reciprocated the Tokyo summit in its own style. On April 25, 10 days after Clinton arrived in Tokyo for the summit, Chinese president Jiang Zemin met Russian president Boris Yeltsin in Beijing. The two leaders announced a decision to establish the Sino-Russian "strategic partnership" and agreed to set up the Sino-Russo Friendship, Peace, and Development Commission. In their bilateral communiqué, the two governments reiterated the policy of de-targeting each other with strategic nuclear weapons (this principle was reached between the two sides in September 1994), proposed to reduce military forces along their common border, and agreed to consolidate their military cooperation. Apparently with the March Taiwan crisis in mind, the two sides emphasized the principle of One China with Taiwan as part of China (*Renmin Ribao,* Apr. 26, 1996: 1). On April 26, China, Russia, and three other former Soviet republics signed an agreement in Shanghai on military trust along their border areas (*Renmin Ribao,* Apr. 27, 1996: 1).

The timing of the Sino-Russian summit was so close to the Tokyo summit that Beijing was willing to imply the connection between the two meetings. On April 19, Jiang said that the Beijing and Shanghai agreements would be a great achievement not only for the signatories but also for Asia-Pacific regional mutual trust (*Renmin Ribao,* Apr. 20, 1996: 1). Scholars at Fudan University in Shanghai were more open about the purpose of the Beijing and Shanghai agreements as a response to the Tokyo summit and suggested that Tokyo and Washington should have received the message.[2] This is the second round of negative reciprocal behavior, in which all three countries attempted to gain foreign support for themselves. Yet, this time, the military hostility did not prevail after the Taiwan crisis; rather, the state leaders resorted to diplomatic warnings as a reciprocal means.

Concerning the Tokyo summit, elements other than the Taiwan crisis could also have shaped the U.S.-Japanese-Chinese reciprocity. Factors such as different political values and domestic pressure may have stimulated hostile reactions, but their impact was not as direct and immediate as the behavior of the three countries during the Taiwan crisis. A fourth country, Russia, did play an external or indirect role in the U.S.-Japanese-Chinese triangle; but the China-Russia summit was the result rather than the cause of Chinese reaction. In short, there is a direct link between the Taiwan crisis and the Tokyo summit.

Finally, we analyze how China, Japan, and the United States interacted with one another during the September-October Diaoyu/Senkaku dispute and how their behavior reciprocated the behavior in the previous events—the Taiwan crisis and the Tokyo summit.

After the March Taiwan crisis, both the Japanese public and the

Japanese government took a tougher view of China. According to a poll conducted between July 25 and August 1, 1996, 71 percent of respondents viewed China's continued military buildup to be threatening Japan's security. (Other threats included a North Korean invasion of South Korea— 61 percent, oil supply—58 percent, Chinese attack on Taiwan—56 percent, Chinese use of force over Senkaku—54 percent, etc.) (*Opinion Analysis,* Sept. 11, 1996: 5). In July, the Japan Defense Agency's annual White Paper, citing China's military buildup and its military exercises over Taiwan in March, listed China as a regional threat for the first time (*Defense News,* July 29–Aug. 4, 1996: 28). Thus in Japan both opinion and policy were responding to earlier Chinese behavior.

As far as Senkaku is concerned, on May 10, Prime Minister Hashimoto renewed Japanese territorial claims and called the islands "indigenous to our nation" (FBIS-EAS, May 10, 1996: 12). On June 7, the Japanese Diet declared a 200–nautical-mile economic zone, which covers the Senkaku islands (FBIS-EAS, June 7, 1996: 12). Previous events resulted in Japan's assertive action. First, the PLA's March exercises had alarmed Japan and sent a signal that China could also resort to force over the Diaoyu/ Senkaku dispute. Second, the April Tokyo summit was welcomed by Japan because it believed that the United States would come to its aid if Japan and China fought over the disputed islands. In general, Japan appeared adamant during the heated tension with China in September and October.

At the same time, China's attitude was strong, and the PLA even conducted large military exercises aimed at the Diaoyu islands. China's reaction might have come from domestic public pressure and a military leadership that urged a firm foreign policy. But more directly, China had reevaluated the U.S.-Japanese alliance because of the Taiwan crisis and the April Tokyo summit. The harsh reaction by the Chinese military in September and October exactly reciprocated Japanese behavior in the March Taiwan crisis and the April summit. On August 22, when Japanese deputy chief of defense Naoaki Murata visited China, Chinese defense minister Chi Haotian said, "I'm afraid of the Japanese-U.S. security arrangement overstepping its bilateral nature." Referring to the PLA's military exercises in March, Chi said that "other countries can say nothing concerning exercises held in our territory or over our territorial waters and air space" (FBIS-EAS, Aug. 22, 1996: 16).

The U.S. reaction to the Diaoyu/Senkaku dispute is the most interesting part of the entire issue. There are several important dynamics for the U.S. non-action: long-term national security concerns in East

Asia, Chinese and Japanese behaviors during the Taiwan crisis and the April Tokyo summit, and other events before and during the September–October Beijing-Tokyo dispute.

The U.S. non-action reciprocated previous Japanese and Chinese behaviors. A restrained Japanese military commitment to the U.S.-Japan alliance during previous events might have modified the U.S. commitment to Japan. In other words, the United States took measured and reciprocal steps toward Japan over the Diaoyu/Senkaku dispute; as a result, the United States made no announcement and took no action in favor of Japan. As for China, the United States already encountered the most serious confrontation with it in decades in March; China, after all, conducted war games, not actual military campaigns against Taiwan. There was no reason for the United States to escalate the tension or pick another fight with China. But there also was no reason for the United States to reward China's previous hostile actions or to lose Japan's trust. This rationale perhaps explains the U.S. neutral or non-action behavior toward the dispute over the Diaoyu/Senkaku islands.

In sum, there had been some negative reciprocal behaviors among the three great powers in 1996. What must be emphasized is that all negative behaviors were greatly self-restrained. For instance, China's military exercises were announced well ahead of time and did not go beyond the designated scope; at the peak of the crisis, Beijing assured Washington that the PLA would not invade Taiwan. For its part, the United States sent two aircraft carrier combat groups near Taiwan but never entered the Taiwan Strait or committed itself to the defense of Taiwan. At the same time, the U.S. government insisted on continued positive engagement with the PLA (Lord 1996).

Nor did the Tokyo summit seek revenge against China, or map out a strategy to contain China, as many speculated it would. Rather, Clinton and Hashimoto issued a quite positive statement about China and announced their intention to cooperate with it. Thus, it is reasonable to argue that the Tokyo summit's cooperative initiative also reciprocated China's military exercises, which did not escalate into a military attack in March. As reported later, immediately after the April Tokyo summit, the U.S. Department of Defense sent officials to brief the matter to the Chinese leadership in Beijing. Japan did not know about the event until September (*Ta Kung Pao,* Mar. 29, 1998: A2)

Just as the Tokyo summit was not decisively aimed at the containment of China, the Beijing summit was not used as a counter-balance against the U.S.-Japan alliance for the long term. There is no evidence that China was ready to unite with Russia to oppose Japan and the United

States. In reality, both China and Russia wished to develop better relations with Japan and the United States.[3]

The same kind of restrained behavior also appeared during the Diaoyu/Senkaku dispute in 1996. Despite all the suspicion and friction, Beijing and Tokyo did not suspend their high-level meetings. In April, Chinese foreign minister Qian visited Tokyo. Japanese deputy chief of defense Murata visited China in August, the highest-level Japanese-Chinese military contact since 1988. On November 8, Japanese foreign minister Ikeda expressed that despite the dispute over Diaoyu/Senkaku, Tokyo was determined to maintain and enhance its relations with China. He went on to say that "basically, bilateral relations with China are as important as those with the United States" (Internet FBIS-EAS, Nov. 12, 1996). Clearly, neither Japan nor China wished to see a breakup of the relationship. Suspicions and disputes did not build up into a strategy of animosity. This way, restrained responses reciprocated previous restrained actions by both governments.

Concerning the U.S. behavior during the Diaoyu/Senkaku dispute, there are notable dynamics explaining the U.S. non-action, especially its restrained and even somewhat positive gesture toward China. After the Taiwan crisis and before the Diaoyu/Senkaku dispute, Sino-U.S. relations experienced subtle changes. Frictions continued as the United States sold anti-aircraft missiles to Taiwan (*Defense News,* Aug. 26–Sept. 1, 1996: 2), and China reportedly assisted Pakistan in building a ballistic missile factory (*New York Times,* Aug. 27, 1996: A6). Meanwhile, however, Beijing was also sending out cooperative signals. On July 29, Beijing issued a statement on halting nuclear tests, which Washington had desired for the worldwide CTBT. A *Beijing Review* commentary stated that "the Chinese government and people are ready to join the governments and people around the world for the realization of this lofty goal" (Aug. 19–25, 1996: 5). On October 10, a Chinese Foreign Ministry spokesman announced the Sino-U.S. consensus on detargeting each other with strategic nuclear weapons despite the absence of a written agreement on such measure (Internet FBIS-CHI, Oct. 15, 1996). In the same month, China endorsed the statement by the United Nations Security Council expressing its "serious concern" about the intrusion of a North Korean submarine into the South Korean territory (Internet New York Times, Oct. 16, 1996). Thus, the U.S. neutral position or non-action over the Diaoyu/Senkaku dispute also took place amid the trend of thawing Sino-U.S. relations; the United States partly reciprocated the Chinese behavior, which included halting nuclear testing and moving to be more cooperative on security dialogue with the United States.

OTHER RECIPROCAL BEHAVIORS

In August 1991, Japanese prime minister Toshiki Kaifu arrived in Beijing as the first state leader from an industrial country to visit China since the 1989 Tiananmen incident. In October 1992, Emperor Akihito was the first Japanese monarch to visit China in history. In turn, Beijing supported Japan's political and military initiatives in East and Southeast Asia. For example, China favored an improved Japanese–North Korean tie and endorsed the dispatch of Japanese peacekeeping troops to Cambodia. Japan and China, together with other countries, virtually cooperated on a common security mission in Cambodia (Zhang 1995: 125).

When President Jiang Zemin visited the United States in November 1997, Prime Minister Hashimoto welcomed the U.S.-China summit as a contribution to the stability of the Asia-Pacific region (Internet FBIS-CHI, Oct. 28, 1997). Similarly, when President Yeltsin visited Japan in April 1998, China applauded the warming Russo-Japanese relationship (Internet FBIS-CHI, Apr. 23, 1998).

U.S.-China relations also reciprocated at a global level. In 1992, the United States decided to sell 150 F-16 fighters to Taiwan. The next year, China boycotted the Middle East arms control talks in protest. In March 1995, Taiwanese leader Lee Teng-hui visited the United States; China immediately broke off talks on the MTCR and cancelled military visits to the United States. China also resorted to arms sales and possible missile/nuclear technology transfer to Iran and Pakistan in retaliation.

At the same time, the United States and China reciprocated and cooperated on the Korean peninsula. In 1994, China supported the United States to achieve the Nuclear Agreed Framework. In 1998, North and South Korea, the United States, and China for the first time conducted four-party talks in an effort to promote stability on the peninsula and continuing implementation of the 1994 Nuclear Agreed Framework.

SUMMARY

A new strategic triangle comprised of the United States, China, and Japan has emerged in the 1990s. This study describes the existence of the triad through one party's impact on the bilateral relationship of the other two parties. The three case studies—the Taiwan crisis, the Tokyo summit, and the Diaoyu/Senkaku dispute—constitute the evidence on the triangular system. The findings demonstrate that whereas China and the United States respectively exercised strong influence on the bilateral relationship between the other two countries, Japan's impact was moderate. However, our knowledge of this triad remains limited; the three-party relationship will continue to evolve as it approaches the twenty-first century.

This study also illustrates the reciprocal behavioral pattern within the triad, by which each country reacts to other countries' previous behavior in kind. In general, all three countries have taken measured and predictable actions during their interaction. Specifically, there are three important findings derived from the study of the behavioral pattern of the strategic triangle.

First, an ad hoc and implicit two-against-one trilateral relationship did appear during the Taiwan crisis and the Tokyo summit. Nevertheless, the two-against-one behavior pattern did not persist even through 1996. The United States, for instance, took a neutral stand over the Sino-Japanese dispute over the Diaoyu/Senkaku islands. Moreover, even the ad hoc hostile actions were very restrained. Understandably suspecting a U.S.-Japan alliance against China, the Chinese did not reach such a conclusion or develop a long-term counter-strategy.[4]

Second, all three powers, despite frictions, did not hesitate to initiate cooperative actions. Cabinet-level meetings between the three governments continued even during the Taiwan crisis and Diaoyu/Senkaku dispute. Instead of perpetuating a two-against-one triangle, the three countries strove to improve the transparency and cooperation within the triad. Positive behavior also was reciprocated.

Third, the reciprocal rather than the two-against-one framework produces a more accurate analysis of the behavior among the three great powers. In particular, as indicated in this article, as hostility failed to prevail, restrained reactions reciprocated restrained actions. A reciprocal model considers both hostile and cooperative actions and therefore leaves an opportunity open for an improved relationship. A two-against-one model presumes a negative cycle of a trilateral relationship and excludes positive evidence and development. Because of this, traditional realism cannot fully interpret a more complex triad such as that of the United States, China, and Japan.

A reciprocal way of thinking is also balanced and appropriate in its policymaking. In this way of thinking, it is probable that the U.S.-Chinese-Japanese triangle may not develop into a hostile confrontation. At the same time, reciprocity provokes the policymakers in the three capitals to appreciate that a negative policy behavior will evoke a similar kind of response.

NOTES

1. This argument was confirmed by Winston Lord in his testimony before the U.S. Congress, "The United States and the Security of Taiwan." See *U.S. Department of State Dispatch,* March 25, 1996: 151.
2. Personal interviews in June 1996 and May 1997.
3. For instance, both Chinese president Jiang Zemin and U.S. president Bill Clinton attempted to establish a strategic partnership in 1997. See *Wen Wei Po,* August 11, 1997: A3.
4. For a balanced analysis, see Duan Tang, "China-U.S.-Japan Triangle: A Critical Relationship," *Beijing Review,* April 7–13, 1997: 7–8. Acknowledging that the United States and Japan may coordinate their strategies in some instances on containing China, Duan suggests that "a breakaway Japan, however, is bound to arouse suspicion and a warning from the United States. . . ." and "There is no way for the triangle to evolve into an alliance between Washington and Tokyo against China. . . ."

6

Conclusion:
Back to the Theory and Future

This book has two purposes: a study of the nature of the U.S.-China-Japan strategic triangle and an exploration of behavioral patterns of this triangle. In this final chapter, we evaluate the research methods for this study, summarize research results, and project future scenarios of the triangle. In the next two decades, we argue, the United States will be a crucial player within the triangle, and its response to the formation of the triangle will largely determine the outcome of Asia-Pacific regional security.

EVALUATION AND SUMMARY

We have applied a three-level analysis—an integrated perceptional, domestic, and international approach. By this method, we have examined how various factors at each level affect the foreign behavior of the three major powers. The distribution of power at the international level has a durable impact on and constitutes a dynamic in adjusting a country's foreign policy; yet, the shifting balance of power between countries does not immediately or decisively determine how a country will behave (whether it will cooperate or confront). Only after decision makers become aware of and adapt to the change of power in a new policy will the distribution of power affect the country's foreign behavior. In other words, because the change of power can take place to any degree and in any direction, decision makers have to decide whether and how to respond to the new distribution of power at the international level. Decision makers also have to consider other countries' intentions and policies, and therefore to develop their own perceptions. At the same time, domestic factors maintain their own trend of development, which may constrain or stimulate a country's behavior. Thus, all factors at the three levels work simultaneously to affect a country's behavior from different directions. In a typical practice, after the process of policy making and thought, a government conducts foreign behavior, responding to the evolving distribution of power and domestic influence. This three-level approach has been applied to the three bilateral relationships in this book in assessing the complex nature of the strategic triangle.

The triadic behavior could follow many kinds of patterns. Confined by the existing evidence, we have adopted the reciprocal model into this study. We closely probe the interaction between the three countries and find that the three parties reciprocate in kind through a series of events. Reciprocity is significantly different from a stereotypical "two-against-one" behavioral pattern. Great powers do not necessarily behave as if they are in a constant state of conflict; rather, they act and react in kind and take measured responses. The reciprocal model is confirmed in this project.

We now review the three pairs of bilateral relations and the reciprocity within the triad. The U.S.-China relationship is the most fragile and vulnerable among the dyads, and has been besieged by issues ranging from human rights, to trade deficit, and to arms proliferation. The Taiwan issue, however, largely forecasts the ups and downs of the changing journey of Sino-U.S. relations, as evidenced by the 1995-96 Taiwan turbulence. China still adheres to a possible use of force on Taiwan; a tide of anti-U.S. sentiment has arisen in China in response to the U.S. intervention in the Taiwan issue by sending aircraft carriers and selling arms. In the United States, domestic forces and the administration are still committed to security around Taiwan; the support for Taiwan has become more vocal, if not necessarily more substantial.

Adding to the Taiwan issue, the dispute over human rights will linger on the Sino-U.S. relationship at least in the near term. The 15th CCP Congress in Beijing did not indicate that the Tiananmen incident will be reinterpreted. It seems that political openness in China will evolve only at a slow pace. By contrast, American human rights activists view an improved civil society in China as a precondition for a normal Sino-U.S. relationship. They will press the U.S. administration for tangible concessions from Beijing. In this regard, Congress will be a source of support for a tough China policy, the media will continue to portray a ruthless Chinese regime, and the public will judge the Sino-U.S. relationship largely from the rights perspective.

That said, we must not overlook the endurance of Sino-U.S. relations. After all, China is becoming a worldwide economic and military power, and the two countries are becoming increasingly interdependent in all issue areas. Economic policy and performance in either country will inevitably affect daily life in the other. Economy has bound the two big countries despite their different ideologies and civilizations. The two governments also have, to a great extent, found common ground on regional tensions, such as North-South Korean relations, nuclear nonproliferation, and even the Taiwan issue. Despite the considerable potential for some kind of Sino-U.S. clash over the Taiwan issue, the two major powers will likely endeavor to evade such a nightmare and continue to collaborate on other similarly crucial security issues, such as nuclear nonproliferation and energy supply around the world.

The U.S.-Japan alliance has entered a new stage of development. Tokyo tends to take a multilateral and more independent military policy into the twenty-first century while maintaining the security alliance with the United States. The U.S. leadership more vigorously presses for the continuation of the alliance and regards it as the cornerstone for Asia-Pacific security and stability. It is the elite perception and official policies in both governments that energize the bilateral military commitment. At present, with the emerging new political and security order in East Asia, Japan is not fully prepared for a self-defense capability. It needs some time to identify its international status. Before the international order matures, Japan's optimal security means remains to be the alliance with the United States. For its part, Washington would like to maintain its presence in East Asia for various economic and security reasons, which mandate the existence of the alliance.

In 1997, the alliance changed its mission from the traditional anti-Soviet focus to an Asia-Pacific-wide security approach. What this new mission means remains to be tested and assessed in the future. Conceivably, the U.S.-Japan alliance has a multifaceted mission—it deters outside military provocations that could jeopardize Asia-Pacific security, but also precludes the occurrence of a militarist Japan.

What has become clear is that in Japan both government and domestic elements have cast some doubt on the continuation of the Japan-U.S. alliance. It would take endless efforts for both Tokyo and Washington to tackle issues such as military bases and defense burden-sharing. Meanwhile, the distribution of power between the United States and Japan adds another uncertain variable on the future alliance. In general, the bilateral alliance is shifting toward a quite different stage, in which common security interests co-exist with other concerns.

The Sino-Japanese relationship has deteriorated since 1994 as both countries have resorted to semi-and indirect military actions over various issues. One cause is the increasing military power on the two sides that has concerned leaderships in both Beijing and Tokyo. Conventional forces of Japan have led all Asian nations in technology and readiness, among which, Aegis destroyers and F-2 fighters are symbolic of Japan's naval and air force predominance. China's strength lies in its strategic nuclear power and its number of personnel and weapons. In the future, China will focus more on quality of its forces, and the balance of power between the two countries will be measured accordingly.

Officials and analysts in both countries have intensified mutual suspicion and treated each other as potential threats. This has been confounded by Japan's fear of China's rising power and China's memory of World War II. Domestic factors also have reached a point that could further the declining trend of the tie. The generation change in both countries has developed against an improved relationship. The traditionally implicit relationship appears to be more explicit in both words and deeds.

Nevertheless, precautions have not caused either country to choose a hostile policy. Diversified national interests and domestic concerns, such as economic growth, have justified a cooperative relationship between the two governments. A confrontation is by no means imminent. Further, the bilateral tension tends to be easing, especially in the context of the U.S.-China-Japan triangle. In other words, the U.S. policy toward Japan and China could determine peace or war between Japan and China, and, therefore, between the three major powers.

In sum, the nature of the strategic triangle is complex and evolving, but relatively stable. All pairs of bilateral relations feature uncertainties, yet no relationship within the triad can be characterized as hostile. Overall, the three powers prefer compromise to stalemate, cooperation to confrontation.

In examining the behavioral pattern of the triad, we have derived three generalizations. First, the three powers have not pursued a two-against-one game. China refuses to align with any other major power; the

United States and Japan also refrain from directing the alliance against China. Second, each power reciprocates the other powers' previous behavior; all three powers respond in kind, positively or negatively. Third, each power takes measured and restrained steps in its interaction with the others; no power overacts or overreacts. Overall, the behavioral pattern has been relatively predictable.

In 1998, the U.S.-China-Japan triangle indicated some new signs. Both the United States and Japan were upbeat about improving relations with China. Japan seemed particularly concerned that the U.S.-China relationship would overshadow the Japan-U.S. relationship. As one Japanese official said, if the situation persists, Japan's influence on Asian security will further decline (Internet FBIS-CHI, Nov. 13, 1997; Jan. 21, 1998).

The existence of the U.S.-Japan alliance within the triad is worth more discussion. In that regard, this strategic triangle would resemble a classic hostile triangle. In the 1990s, however, the alliance seems to have played a rather constructive role in stabilizing the U.S.-Japan-China triad and preventing the triad from evolving into a two-against-one hostile game. At present, Japan is satisfied with the defense protection provided by the alliance and forgoes building a strategic-offensive system. China is suspicious of the U.S.-Japan alliance but does not try to undo it. China understands that the alliance is in the interests of other Asian nations and helps keep Japan under control. Thus, China chooses to limit rather than eliminate the alliance. For the United States, the alliance renders the Sino-Japanese arms race unnecessary and brings stability to East Asia. The United States also finds Japan to be an indispensable hosting country for its major military deployment in the West Pacific.

SCENARIOS

This book projects three possible types of triangular relationships in the next 20 years. First, the triangle might become more visible, transparent, and cooperative. Second, the triangle might evolve into a hostile relationship. Third, the triangle might loosen or dissolve into a more complex and multilateral framework.

A Transparent Triangle

In the future, the U.S.-China-Japan strategic triad could mature and become more visible. In this scenario, each country would clearly influence the bilateral relationship between the other two countries; each bilateral relationship would influence the behavior of a third party; and the three dyads would influence each other. As this pattern of triangle became tangible, and if each side continued its restrained behavior, the three parties would handle their issues and differences in a more transparent and cooperative manner. As a result, a pattern of benign trilateral security dialogue would emerge and greatly enhance regional security and stability. It is encouraging to note that as Chinese president Jiang was visiting Washington in October 1997, Japanese prime minister Hashimoto called the event conducive to the stability of the Asia-Pacific region. Officials in the United States, China, and Japan now all believe that trilateral security dialogue should be conducted at least at a track-two (unofficial) level.

A Hostile Triangle

A hostile triangle will materialize if any party goes too far and takes extreme provocative action. In this scenario and in a descendant order of likelihood, a hostile triad could emerge as a U.S.-Japan alliance against China, a U.S.-China alliance against Japan, or a China-Japan alliance against the United States. The scenario could also be a two-against-two game; for example, a U.S.-Japan alliance against a China-Russia alliance. It is worth noting that as the United States and Japan have tightened their alliance in recent years, China and Russia have developed a closer military tie. Although Beijing is not interested in revitalizing a Sino-Russo military alliance at the moment, a U.S.-Japan alliance aimed at China could force Chinese leaders to evoke this as a final resort. This pattern of security relations would undoubtedly be the most devastating one.

A Loosening Triangle

The triad could become less visible and gradually lose its triangular focus; over time it could evolve into a more diversified and multilateral framework of international relations. As nations become more interdependent, the three countries in question may not find a triangular formula to be the most dynamic and helpful mechanism for pursuing national interests. Rather, they may be diverted by issues and attracted by organizations beyond the triad; consequently, they might become integrated into a multilateral forum although they may still handle some issues through a triangular framework.

In the next few years, however, none of the three scenarios will predominate. The triangle will continue to transform under its current emerging and ambiguous image, whose change is driven by elite perceptions, domestic development, and the distribution of power in the international system.

In a medium term, all three scenarios are possible, depending upon how perceptions, domestic factors, and the distribution of power have shifted. Whereas a transparent triangle is the most desirable, as the triangle continues to exist, a loosening triangle is more likely in the future.

Therefore, from a policy perspective, it is advisable for all three governments to pursue a transparent and reciprocal triangular tie. A collaborative triad would benefit each side to a maximum degree. The key player, as we suggested in previous chapters, is the United States. This is because the United States is more powerful in both a military and an economic dimension, and is expected to be a neutral player in the triad. The United States could determine the nature of the triad to a larger extent than any other country.

THE ROLE OF THE UNITED STATES

For the sake of a stable triad, the United States should clearly understand the nature of Sino-Japanese relations, which is studied least in the United States compared to what is available on U.S. relations with other countries. First, the Sino-Japanese tie will not break up although it has experienced tensions and frictions. The two countries still depend upon each other both economically and politically; a Sino-Japanese hostility that requires the United States to take sides is remote. We have elaborated this thrust in chapter 4. Second, the Sino-Japanese tie will not become so close as to threaten the U.S. interests in East Asia. This possibility is unlikely in the next 20 years, during which the Sino-Japanese relationship will become more competitive for both economic opportunities and political influence. At the same time, both China and Japan will rely on a favorable U.S. position regarding their pursuit of national and international interests. Essentially, a reliable relationship with the United States will serve them; a worsened relationship with the United States will place the two Asian countries under a heavy strain. Third, despite an ally, Japan will not be readily called upon by the United States in a major conflict. Domestic Japanese resistance to a major war with China or use of force overseas should not be underestimated. We have probed this issue in previous chapters but more pointedly in chapter 5. We believe that such an overall assessment of Sino-Japanese relations constitutes a crucial basis for an agile U.S. strategy in the early twenty-first century.

Counting the two major Asian powers separately, China remains a myth, a puzzle, a trouble, or even a threat to some in the United States. The United States has gradually and partially started to learn about China. As described in a group report by the American Assembly at Columbia University, "Few Americans have an accurate understanding of the complexity of the internal situation in China or of the extraordinary pace and consequences of its rapid change" (American Assembly, 1996: 8). Among all the debates on China, its rising national power and its ability and willingness to use force in particular have been distinct questions. At present, the consensus has been reached among many in the United States that China is an emerging world power and will somewhat redraw the landscape of international politics. Beyond that, however, profound differences remain about a long-term U.S. China policy.

We assess China as an emerging world power in the next twenty years along the following lines. First, there will be periodical political, economic, ethnic, and social turbulence within China. Prominent possibilities are political power redistribution within and eventually outside the Chinese Communist Party; central-local relations; continued market economic reforms and their consequent shock waves across private and particularly state-owned sectors; ethnic activities in Tibet, Xinjiang and other bordering areas against the Beijing regime; and social frustrations caused by economic adjustments, rising crime, and declining moral standards.

Second, in parallel with these unstable factors, China will continue to increase its economic power, modernize its military forces, and integrate into the world economic and political system. China will certainly become more democratic and economically market-oriented; yet China may not change to fit into a Western political or cultural model.

Finally, China will naturally expand its political, economic, and military influence in the world. Foremost, China will strive to achieve and maintain unification with Hong Kong, Macau, and Taiwan, and to a lesser extent, secure some kind of control over parts of the South China Sea islands. Beyond these traditional Chinese claims, however, there is no reason to believe that China will become a revisionist state or an evil empire that seeks to grab other countries' territory. Achieving its traditional claims over Taiwan will prove too formidable for China; a complicated domestic situation and limited projection power will only constrain any assertive Chinese behavior.

President Clinton pronounced in his February 4, 1997 State of the Union Address that "engaging China is the best way to work on common challenges like ending nuclear testing—as to deal frankly with fundamental differences like human rights" (Internet *New York Times*, Feb. 5,

1997). Many also have called for developing a more cooperative overall relationship with China to advance mutual interests. A consistent, steady, bipartisan, and long-term U.S. China policy is considered to be at stake (Zoellick, 1996/97). For that purpose, some have proposed to focus first on building cooperation in areas where common interests converge, and then to make progress in solving more difficult problems (American Assembly, 1996: 11). At the October 1997 summit in Washington, Clinton's China policy seemed to partially succeed. President Clinton and President Jiang Zemin agreed to establish a hotline between the two capitals, signed a pact on cooperation in peaceful use of nuclear energy, and vowed to observe nuclear nonproliferation norms and fight against international crimes; at the same time, they frankly and openly exchanged different views on human rights. In June 1998, President Clinton and Jiang Zemin held their Beijing summit which sought to establish a strategic partnership.

Nevertheless, the U.S. China policy can be complicated and disputed in a broader policy context, for example, within the U.S.-China-Japan triangle. This should not be a surprise because there traditionally has been competition between China policy and Japan policy in the United States.

In the 1990s, it is not rare to hear some officials and analysts saying that the U.S.-Japan alliance should be operated to prevent the rise of a powerful China. They hope that the TMD and the review of the U.S.-Japan Defense Cooperation Guidelines can be a vehicle to contain China. But some argued that "a war with China would almost certainly bankrupt the United States, radicalize China, and tear Japan apart" (Johnson 1996: 12). Thus, others suggested that a more efficient U.S. Asia policy is to balance Japan and China against each other (Layne 1997).

Kent Calder implies that in the Asia-Pacific region China is the problem and Japan is the solution. He argues that "it is both foolish and dangerous to depreciate China or to doubt its long-term potential. Yet that very potential could well be threatening for other nations, including U.S. Pacific allies like Japan . . ." (Calder 1996: 216). He continues that "in building bridges to China, the United States must be very careful not to neglect Japan" (217). He does emphasize that the way to stabilize the vital Pacific triangle is "not for the United States to shift deftly from one side to the other between China and Japan" (217). Above all, however, Calder poses that the United States should sharpen the U.S.-Japan alliance to solve crucial problems related to China (201, 217). Thus, "Japan First" appeals to some U.S. policy-thinkers. Before President Clinton took his trip to China in June 1998, American ambassador to

Japan Thomas Foley told Secretary of State Albright and the White House that the administration's China policy should not come at the expense of Japan (*New York Times*, Apr. 29, 1998: 6).

Indeed, Japan is different from China in many ways. Japan is a democracy, has a more developed economy, contains greater military and technological potential, and has been a consistent U.S. ally from the early 1950s. These elements qualify Japan as a key U.S. ally and serve both countries' interests. On this basis, the U.S.-Japan alliance has a good reason to continue for a long time. Japan, however, is also different from the United States. Although Japan is allied strategically with the United States, it is also an Asian nation and the historical and cultural ties between the two countries, as well as nation-to-nation mutual trust and understanding, are weak or even destructible. Weaknesses within the alliance aside, Japan is a morally crippled ally in Asia, and its reluctance to acknowledge its World War II crimes does not favor the health of the U.S.-Japan alliance. In May 1998, Japan released a movie, "Pride, the Fateful Moment," which depicts General Hideki Tojo, the wartime prime minister, as a patriot and gentle family man. As a *Washington Post* critic commented, "fifty years after war, a remarkable perception gap still exists between Japan and the rest of the world" (May 25, 1998: B4).

In short, the United States, China, and Japan differ from each other. Difference does not necessarily mean conflict or deny the possibility of collaboration. A long-term U.S. Asia policy ought not to rely on conflict between countries. Considering that both China and Japan are different from the United States, however, the United States should pursue different strategies towards the two Asian nations. It is particularly noteworthy that the fear and tension between China and Japan stem from emotions of a different era. "Never before have China and Japan both been powerful at the same time" (Mahbubani 1997: 152). A sound U.S. strategy should consider the following elements.

First, the United States should not push a U.S.-Japan alliance for an anti-China purpose, which, as analyzed earlier, would trigger a conflict involving the three and could even extend to include other countries. At present, to pursue any kind of anti-China strategy would only prove to be unnecessary, costly, and even counterproductive.

Second, due to current varying understandings of critical security issues such as Taiwan, the United States cannot build a genuine alliance or partnership with China, and should focus on a positive bilateral working relationship. Confidence and trust need to be restored before anything else. As a new strategic step, however, the United States should develop and maintain a partnership with China in the long term. This would not be an equal-distance strategy versus Japan. Rather, from the U.S. perspective, its China policy should have a similar mission of the U.S.-Japan alliance: the United States cannot overcome any major Asia-Pacific security problems without cooperation with China; a stable partnership with China will not only essentially favor U.S. national interests but also contribute to peace and stability in the world. In this regard, the U.S.-China partnership is just another pillar of the entire U.S. Asia strategy, and the mission is doable.

Finally, the United States should not terminate the U.S.-Japan alliance, which will continue to play a positive role if properly managed. The alliance should first of all safeguard Japanese security and U.S. interests in Asia, but turn away from intensifying intra-Asian conflict. In this regard, the triad is important. China can be counted on to help establish a new architecture for Asia-Pacific security, and the U.S.-China relationship should play a more important role than other bilateral relationships.

The ultimate goal of the U.S. strategy should be a transparent and cooperative U.S.-China-Japan triangle. It is in the long-term U.S. interests to foster confidence and trust in East Asia. At the same time, the United States should explore multilateral approaches to national interests and multilateral issues. This requires the United States to look beyond not only bilateral alliances but also trilateral interactions.

Appendix 1

Remarks by President Clinton in His Address on China and the National Interest

The White House
Office of the Press Secretary
October 24, 1997
(Voice of America, Washington, D.C.)

Thank you very much, Ambassador Platt. I thank the Asia Society and the U.S.-China Education Foundation for bringing us together today. I thank Senator Baucus and Congressmen Dreier, Matsui, and Roemer for being here; Secretary Albright, Ambassador Barshefsky, National Security Advisor Berger, the other distinguished officials from the State Department. And I thank especially the members of the diplomatic corps who are here, and the students. And especially let me thank two of my favorite people, Joe Duffy and Evelyn Lieberman, for the work of the Voice of America and the USIA, all that they do to promote the free flow of ideas around the world.

Next week, when President Jiang Zemin comes to Washington, it will be the first state visit by a Chinese leader to the United States for more than a decade. The visit gives us the opportunity and the responsibility to chart a course for the future that is more positive and more stable and, hopefully, more productive than our relations have been for the last few years.

China is a great country with a rich and proud history and a strong future. It will, for good or ill, play a very large role in shaping the 21st century in which the children in this audience today, children all across our country, all across China, and indeed all across the world, will live.

At the dawn of the new century, China stands at a crossroads. The direction China takes toward cooperation or conflict will profoundly affect Asia, America, and the world for decades. The emergence of a China as a power that is stable, open, and non-aggressive, that embraces free markets, political pluralism, and the rule of law, that works with us to build a secure international order—that kind of China, rather than a China turned inward and confrontational, is deeply in the interests of the American people.

Of course, China will choose its own destiny. Yet by working with China and expanding areas of cooperation, dealing forthrightly with our differences, we can advance fundamental American interests and values.

First, the United States has a profound interest in promoting a peaceful, prosperous, and stable world. Our task will be much easier if China is a part of that process—not only playing by the rules of international behavior, but helping to write and enforce them.

China is a permanent member of the United Nations Security Council. Its support was crucial for peacekeeping efforts in Cambodia and building international mandates to reverse Iraq's aggression against Kuwait and restore democracy to Haiti. As a neighbor of India and Pakistan, China will influence whether these great democracies move toward responsible cooperation both with each other and with China.

From the Persian Gulf to the Caspian Sea, China's need for a reliable and efficient supply of energy to fuel its growth can make it a force for stability in these strategically critical regions. Next week, President Jiang and I will discuss our visions of the future and the kind of strategic relationship we must have to promote cooperation, not conflict.

Second, the United States has a profound interest in peace and stability in Asia. Three times this century, Americans have fought and died in Asian wars—37,000 Americans still patrol the Cold War's last frontier, on the Korean DMZ. Territorial disputes that could flair into crises affecting America require us to maintain a strong American security presence in Asia. We want China to be a powerful force for security and cooperation there.

China has helped us convince North Korea to freeze and ultimately end its dangerous nuclear program. Just imagine how much more dangerous that volatile peninsula would be today if North Korea, reeling from food shortages, with a million soldiers encamped 27 miles from Seoul, had continued this nuclear program.

China also agreed to take part in the four-party peace talks that President Kim and I proposed with North Korea, the only realistic avenue to a lasting peace. And China is playing an increasingly constructive role in Southeast Asia by working with us and the members of ASEAN to advance our shared interests in economic and political security.

Next week I'll discuss with President Jiang the steps we can take together to advance the peace process in Korea. We'll look at ways to strengthen our military-to-military contacts, decreasing the chances of miscalculation and broadening America's contacts with the next generation of China's military leaders. And I will reiterate to President Jiang America's continuing support for our One China policy, which has allowed democracy to flourish in Taiwan, and Taiwan's relationship with the PRC to grow more stable and prosper. The Taiwan question can only be settled by the Chinese themselves peacefully.

Third, the United States has a profound interest in keeping weapons of mass destruction and other sophisticated weapons out of unstable regions and away from rogue states and terrorists. In the 21st century, many of the threats to our security will come not from great power conflict, but from states that defy the international community and violent groups seeking to undermine peace, stability, and democracy. China is already a nuclear power with increasingly sophisticated industrial and technological capabilities. We need its help to prevent dangerous weapons from falling into the wrong hands.

For years, China stood outside the major international arms control regimes. Over the past decade, it has made important and welcome decisions to join the Nuclear Nonproliferation Treaty, the Chemical Weapons Convention, the Biological Weapons Convention, and to respect key provisions of the Missile Technology Control Regime. Last year at the United Nations, I was proud to be the first world leader to sign the Comprehensive Test Ban Treaty. China's foreign minister was the second leader to do so. China has lived up to its pledge not to assist unsafeguarded nuclear facilities in third countries, and it is developing a system of export controls to prevent the transfer or sale of technology for weapons of mass destruction.

But China still maintains some troubling weapons supply relationships. At the summit, I will discuss with President Jiang further steps we hope China will take to end or limit some of these supply relationships and to strengthen and broaden its export control system. And I will make the case to him that these steps are, first and foremost, in China's interest, because the spread of dangerous weapons and technology would increase instability near China's own borders.

Fourth, the United States has a profound interest in fighting drug-trafficking and international organized crime. Increasingly, smugglers and criminals are taking advantage of China's vast territory and its borders with 15 nations to move drugs and weapons, aliens, and the proceeds of illegal activities from one point in Asia to another, or from Asia to Europe.

China and the United States already are cooperating closely on alien smuggling, and China has taken a tough line against narco trafficking, a threat to its children as well as our own. Next week I will propose to President Jiang that our law enforcement communities intensify their efforts together.

Fifth, the United States has a profound interest in making global trade and investment as free, fair, and open as possible. Over the past five years, trade has produced more than one-third of America's economic growth. If we are to continue generating good jobs and higher incomes in our country, when we are just 4 percent of the world's population, we must continue to sell more to the other 96 percent. One of the best ways to do that is to bring China more fully into the world's trading system. With a quarter of the world's population and its fastest-growing economy, China could and should be a magnet for our goods and services.

Even though American exports to China now are at an all-time high, so, too, is our trade deficit. In part, this is due to the strength of the American economy, and to the fact that many products we used to buy in other Asian countries now are manufactured in China. But clearly, an important part of the problem remains lack of access to China's markets.

We strongly support China's admission into the World Trade Organization. But in turn, China must dramatically improve access for foreign goods and services. We should be able to compete fully and fairly in China's marketplace, just as China competes in our own.

Tearing down trade barriers also is good for China, and for the growth of China's neighbors and, therefore, for the stability and future of Asia. Next week, President Jiang and I will discuss steps China must take to join the WTO and assume its rightful place in the world economy.

Finally, the United States has a profound interest in ensuring that today's progress does not come at tomorrow's expense. Greenhouse gas emissions are leading to climate change. China is the fastest-growing contributor to greenhouse gas emissions, and we are the biggest greenhouse gas emitter. Soon, however, China will overtake the United States and become the largest contributor. Already, pollution has made respiratory disease the number-one health problem for China's people. Last March, when he visited China, Vice President Gore launched a joint forum with the Chinese on the environment and development so that we can work with China to pursue growth and protect the environment at the same time.

China has taken some important steps to deal with its need for more energy and cleaner air. Next week, President Jiang and I will talk about the next steps China can take to combat climate change. It is a global problem that must have a global solution that cannot come without China's participation, as well. We also will talk about what American companies and technology can do to support China in its efforts to reduce air pollution and increase clean energy production.

Progress in each of these areas will draw China into the institutions and arrangements that are setting the ground rules for the 21st century—the security partnerships; the open trade arrangements; the arms-control regime; the multinational coalitions against terrorism; crime, and drugs; the commitments to preserve the environment and to uphold human rights. This is our best hope, to secure our own interests and values and to advance China's in the historic transformation that began 25 years ago, when China reopened to the world.

As we all know, the transformation already has produced truly impressive results. Twenty-five years ago, China stood apart from and closed to the international community. Now, China is a member of more than 1,000 international organizations—from the International Civil Aviation Organization to the International Fund for Agricultural Development. It has moved from the 22nd largest trading nation to the 11th. It is projected to become the second-largest trader, after the United States, by 2020. And today, 40,000 young Chinese are studying here in the United States, with hundreds of thousands more living and learning in Europe, Asia, Africa, and Latin America.

China's economic transformation has been even more radical. Market reforms have spurred more than two decades of unprecedented growth, and the decision at the recently ended 15th Party Congress to sell off most all of China's big, state-owned industries promises to keep China moving toward a market economy.

The number of people living in poverty has dropped from 250

million to 58 million, even as China's population has increased by nearly 350 million. Per-capita income in the cities has jumped 550 percent in just the past decade.

As China has opened its economy, its people have enjoyed greater freedom of movement and choice of employment, better schools and housing. Today, most Chinese enjoy a higher standard of living than at any time in China's modern history. But as China has opened economically, political reform has lagged behind.

Frustration in the West turned into condemnation after the terrible events in Tiananmen Square. Now, nearly a decade later, one of the great questions before the community of democracies is how to pursue the broad and complex range of our interests with China while urging and supporting China to move politically as well as economically into the 21st century. The great question for China is how to preserve stability, promote growth, and increase its influence in the world, while making room for the debate and the dissent that are a part of the fabric of all truly free and vibrant societies. The answer to those questions must begin with an understanding of the crossroads China has reached.

As China discards its old economic order, the scope and sweep of change has rekindled historic fears of chaos and disintegration. In return, Chinese leaders have worked hard to mobilize support, legitimize power, and hold the country together, which they see is essential to restoring the greatness of their nation and its rightful influence in the world. In the process, however, they have stifled political dissent to a degree and in ways that we believe are fundamentally wrong, even as freedom from want, freedom of movement, and local elections have increased.

This approach has caused problems within China and in its relationship to the United States. Chinese leaders believe it is necessary to hold the nation together, to keep it growing, to keep moving toward its destiny. But it will become increasingly difficult to maintain the closed political system in an ever-more-open economy and society.

China's economic growth has made it more and more dependent on the outside world for investment, markets, and energy. Last year, it was the second largest recipient of foreign direct investment in the world. These linkages bring with them powerful forces for change. Computers and the Internet, fax machines and photo-copiers, modems and satellites all increase the exposure to people, ideas, and the world beyond China's borders. The effect is only just beginning to be felt.

Today, more than a billion Chinese have access to television, up from just 10 million two decades ago. Satellite dishes dot the landscape. They receive dozens of outside channels, including Chinese language services of CNN, Star TV, and Worldnet. Talk radio is increasingly popular and relatively unregulated in China's 1,000 radio stations. And 70 percent of China's students regularly listen to the Voice of America.

China's 2,200 newspapers, up from just 42 three decades ago, and more than 7,000 magazines and journals are more open in content. A decade ago, there were 50,000 mobile phones in China; now there are more than 7 million. The Internet already has 150,000 accounts in China, with more than a million expected to be online by the year 2000. The more ideas and information spread, the more people will expect to think for themselves, express their own opinions, and participate. And the more that happens, the harder it will be for their government to stand in their way.

Indeed, greater openness is profoundly in China's own interest. If welcomed, it will speed economic growth, enhance the world influence of China, and stabilize society. Without the full freedom to think, question, to create, China will be at a distinct disadvantage, competing with fully open societies in the Information Age where the greatest source of national wealth is what resides in the human mind.

China's creative potential is truly staggering. The largest population in the world is not yet among its top 15 patent powers. In an era where these human resources are what really matters, a country that holds its people back cannot achieve its full potential.

Our belief that, over time, growing interdependence would have a liberalizing effect in China does not mean in the meantime we should or we can ignore abuses in China of human rights or religious freedom. Nor does it mean that there is nothing we can do to speed the process of liberalization.

Americans share a fundamental conviction that people everywhere have the right to be treated with dignity, to give voice to their opinion, to choose their own leaders, to worship as they please. From Poland to South Africa, from Haiti to the Philippines, the democratic saga of the last decade proves that these are not American rights or Western rights or developed-world rights, they are the birthrights of every human being enshrined in the Universal Declaration of Human Rights.

Those who fight for human rights and against religious persecution, at the risk of their jobs, their freedom, even their lives, find strength through knowledge that they are not alone, that the community of democracies stands with them. The United States, therefore, must and will continue to stand up for human rights, to speak out against their abuse in China or anywhere else in the world. To do otherwise would run counter to everything we stand for as Americans. (Applause.)

Over the past year, our State Department's annual human rights report again pulled no punches on China. We cosponsored a resolution critical of China's human rights record in Geneva, even though many of our allies had abandoned the effort. We continue to speak against the arrest of dissidents, and for a resumed dialogue with the Dalai Lama, on behalf of the people and the distinct culture and unique identity of the people of Tibet—not their political independence, but their uniqueness.

We established Radio Free Asia. We are working with Congress to expand its broadcast and to support civil society and the rule of law programs in China. We continue to pursue the problem of prison labor and we regularly raise human rights in all our high-level meetings with the Chinese.

We do this in the hope of a dialogue. And in dialogue we must also admit that we in America are not blameless in our social fabric—our crime rate is too high, too many of our children are still killed with guns, too many of our streets are still riddled with drugs. We have things to learn from other societies as well, and problems we have to solve. And if we expect other people to listen to us about the problems they have, we must be prepared to listen to them about the problems we have.

This pragmatic policy of engagement, of expanding our areas of cooperation with China while confronting our differences openly and respectfully—this is the best way to advance our fundamental interests and our values and to promote a more open and free China.

I know there are those who disagree. They insist that China's interests and America's are inexorably in conflict. They do not believe the Chinese system will continue to evolve in a way that elevates not only human material condition, but the human spirit. They, therefore, believe we should be working harder to contain or even to confront China before it becomes even stronger.

I believe this view is wrong. Isolation of China is unworkable, counterproductive, and potentially dangerous. Military, political, and economic measures to do such a thing would find little support among our allies around the world and, more importantly, even among Chinese themselves working for greater liberty. Isolation would encourage the Chinese to become hostile and to adopt policies of conflict with our own interests and values. It will eliminate, not facilitate, cooperation on weapons proliferation. It would hinder, not help, our efforts to foster stability in Asia. It would exacerbate, not ameliorate, the plight of dissidents. It would close off, not open up, one of the world's most important markets. It would make China less, not more, likely to play by the rules of international conduct and to be a part of an emerging international consensus.

As always, America must be prepared to live and flourish in a world in which we are at odds with China. But that is not the world we want. Our objective is not containment and conflict; it is cooperation. We will far better serve our interests and our principles if we work with a China that shares that objective with us. (Applause.)

Thirty years ago, President Richard Nixon, then a citizen campaigning for the job I now hold, called for a strategic change in our policy toward China. Taking the long view, he said, we simply cannot afford to leave China forever outside the family of nations. There is no place on this small planet for a billion of its potentially most able people to live in angry isolation.

Almost two decades ago, President Carter normalized relations with China, recognizing the wisdom of that statement. And over the past two-and-a-half decades, as China has emerged from isolation; tensions with the West have decreased; cooperation has increased; prosperity has spread to more of China's people. The progress was a result of China's decision to play a more constructive role in the world and to open its economy. It was supported by a far-sighted America policy that made clear to China we welcome its emergence as a great nation.

Now, America must stay on that course of engagement. By working with China and making our differences clear where necessary, we can advance our interests and our values and China's historic transformation into a nation whose greatness is defined as much by its future as its past.

Change may not come as quickly as we would like, but, as our interests are long-term, so must our policies be. We have an opportunity to build a new century in which China takes its rightful place as a full and strong partner in the community of nations, working with the United States to advance peace and prosperity, freedom and security for both our people and for all the world. We have to take that chance.

Thank you very much. (Applause.)

Appendix 2

Remarks by Chinese President Jiang Zemin

News Conference
Washington, D.C.
October 30, 1997
Federal Document Clearing House

Ladies and gentlemen, a while ago, I had an in-depth exchange of views with President Clinton on China-U.S. relations and on international and regional issues of mutual interest. The meeting was constructive and full. President Clinton and I have agreed on identifying the goals for the development of a China-U.S. relationship oriented toward the 21st century. The two sides believe that efforts to realize this goal will promote the fundamental interests of the two peoples and the noble cause of world peace and development.

We both agree that our two countries share extensive common interests in important matters bearing on the survival and development of mankind, such as peace and development, economic cooperation and trade, the prevention of the proliferation of weapons of mass destruction, and environmental protection.

Both sides are of the view that it is imperative to handle China-U.S.

relations and properly address our differences in accordance with the principles of mutual respect, noninterference in each other's internal affairs, equality and mutual benefit, and seeking common ground while putting aside differences.

President Clinton and I have also reached broad agreement on the establishment of a mechanism of regular summit meetings; the opening of a hotline between the two heads of state; the establishment of a mechanism of . . . consultations between the two foreign ministers and other officials; an increase in exchanges between the armed forces of the two countries; and exchanges and cooperation between our two countries in economic, scientific and technological, cultural, educational, and law enforcement fields. My visit will achieve the purpose of enhancing mutual understanding, broadening common ground, developing cooperation, and building a future together, and bring China-U.S. relations into a new stage of development.

President Clinton and I share the view that China and the United States enjoy a high degree of complementarity and a huge potential for cooperation in the economic and trade fields. To step up our economic cooperation in trade not only benefits our two peoples, but also contributes to economic development and prosperity of the world.

And I would also like to take this opportunity to thank you, Mr. President, for the kind reception accorded to me. Now questions are welcome.

Appendix 3

Excerpts of Text of U.S.-Japan Defense Cooperation Guidelines

New York, September 23, 1997, Kyodo
Source: FBIS-EAS

I. THE AIM OF THE GUIDELINES

The aim of these guidelines is to create a solid basis for more effective and credible U.S.-Japan cooperation under normal circumstances, in case of an armed attack against Japan, and in situations in areas surrounding Japan. The guidelines also provide a general framework and policy direction for the roles and missions of the two countries and ways of cooperation and coordination, both under normal circumstances and during contingencies.

II. BASIC PREMISES AND PRINCIPLES

The guidelines and programs under the guidelines are consistent with the following basic premises and principles. The rights and obligations under the treaty of mutual cooperation and security between the United States of America and Japan (the U.S.-Japan Security Treaty) and its related arrangements, as well as the fundamental framework of the U.S.-Japan alliance, will remain unchanged.

Japan will conduct all its actions within the limitations of its constitution and in accordance with such basic positions as the maintenance of its exclusively defense-oriented policy and its three non-nuclear principles.

All actions taken by the United States and Japan will be consistent with basic principles of international law, including the peaceful settlement of disputes and sovereign equality, and relevant international agreements such as the charter of the United Nations.

The guidelines and programs under the guidelines will not obligate either government to take legislative, budgetary, or administrative measures. However, since the objective of the guidelines and programs under the guidelines is to establish an effective framework for bilateral cooperation, the two governments are expected to reflect in an appropriate way the results of these efforts, based on their own judgments, in their specific policies and measures. All actions taken by Japan will be consistent with its laws and regulations then in effect.

III. COOPERATION UNDER NORMAL CIRCUMSTANCES

Both governments will firmly maintain existing U.S.-Japan security arrangements. Each government will make efforts to maintain required defense postures. Japan will possess defense capability within the scope necessary for self-defense on the basis of the "National Defense Program Outline." In order to meet its commitments, the United States will maintain its nuclear-deterrent capability, its forward-deployed forces in the Asia-pacific region, and other forces capable of reinforcing those forward deployed forces.

IV. ACTION IN RESPONSE TO AN ARMED ATTACK AGAINST JAPAN

Bilateral actions in response to an armed attack against Japan remain a core aspect of U.S.-Japan defense cooperation.

When an armed attack against Japan is imminent, the two governments will take steps to prevent further deterioration of the situation and make preparations necessary for the defense of Japan. When an armed attack against Japan takes place, the two governments will conduct appropriate bilateral actions to repel it at the earliest possible stage.

V. COOPERATION IN SITUATIONS IN AREAS SURROUNDING JAPAN

Situations in areas surrounding Japan will have an important influence on Japan's peace and security. The concept, situations in areas surrounding Japan, is not geographic but situational. The two governments will make every effort, including diplomatic efforts, to prevent such situations from occurring. When the two governments reach a common assessment of the state of each situation, they will effectively coordinate their activities. In responding to such situations, measures taken may differ depending on circumstances.

Bibliography

Abe, Hitoshi, Muneyuki Shindo, and Sadafumi Kawato. *The Government and Politics of Japan.* Tokyo: University of Tokyo Press, 1994.

Advisory Group on Defense Issues. *The Modality of the Security and Defense Capability of Japan: Outlook for the 21st Century.* Tokyo: 1994.

Akaha, Tsuneo. "Japan's Security Policy in the Posthegemonic World." In *Japan in the Posthegemonic World,* edited by T. Akaha and Frank Langdom, 91–112. Boulder: Lynne Rienner Publishers, 1993.

Allen, Kenneth, Glenn Krumel, and Jonathan Pollack. *China's Air Force Enters the 21st Century.* Santa Monica: The RAND, 1995.

American Assembly. *China-U.S. Relations in the Twenty-First Century.* New York: Columbia University, 1996.

Arase, David. "Japan in East Asia." In *Japan in the Posthegemonic World,* edited by T. Akaha and Frank Langdom, 113–136. Boulder: Lynne Rienner Publishers, 1993.

Armacost, Michael. *Friends or Rivals? The Insider's Account of U.S.-Japan Relations.* New York: Columbia University Press, 1996.

Ashley, Richard. *The Political Economy of War and Peace.* New York: Nichols Publishing Company, 1980.

Axelrod, Robert. *The Evolution of Cooperation.* New York: Basic Books, 1984.

Baldwin, David, ed. *Neorealism and Neoliberalism: The Contemporary Debate.* New York: Columbia University Press, 1993.

Bandow, Doug. "Keeping the Troops and the Money at Home." *Current History* 93, No. 573 (January 1994): 8–13.

Barnett, A. Doak. *China and the Major Powers in East Asia.* Washington, D.C.: Brookings Institution, 1977.

Benoit, Kenneth. "Democracies Really Are More Pacific (in General)." *Journal of Conflict Resolution* 40, No. 4 (December 1996): 636–657.

Berger, Samuel. "Building a New Consensus on China." Speech at the Council on Foreign Relations, New York, June 6, 1997.

Betts, Richard. "Wealth, Power, and Instability." *International Security* 18, No. 3 (Winter 1993/94): 34–77.

Blaker, Michael. "Japan in 1995: a Year of Natural and Other Disasters." *Asian Survey* 36 No. 1 (January 1996): 41–52.

Blum, Douglas. "The Soviet Foreign Policy Belief System: Beliefs, Politics, and Foreign Policy Outcomes." *International Studies Quarterly* 37, No. 3 (1993): 373–394.

Bobrow, Davis. "Japan in the World: Opinion from Defeat to Success." *Journal of Conflict Resolution* 33, No. 4 (December 1989): 571–604.

Brams, Steven. *Game Theory and Politics.* New York: Free Press, 1975.

Bristow, Damon. "*Osumi* Unlocks Japan's Maritime Potential." *Jane's International Defense Review* 31 (February 1998): 53–56.

Bueno de Mesquita, Bruce, and David Lalman. *War and Reason.* New Haven: Yale University Press, 1992.

CQ Researcher. "Taiwan, China and the U.S." *CQ Researcher* (May 24, 1996): 457–480.

Calder, Kent. *Pacific Defense: Arms, Energy, and America's Future in Asia.* New York: William Morrow and Company, 1996.

Caplow, Theodore. *Two Against One.* Englewood Cliffs, NJ: Prentice-Hall, 1968.

Chang, Gong. "Zouxiang Zhengzhi Junshi Daguo de Zhongyao Buzhou" (Leaping toward a Big Political and Military Power). *Conmilit* 16, No. 7 (November 1992): 52–54.

Chen, Min. *The Strategic Triangle and Regional Conflicts: Lessons from the Indochina War.* Boulder: Lynne Rienner Publishers, 1992.

Chen, Peiyao. "The New Asia-Pacific Triangle of Dependence, Constraint, Cooperation, and Competition." *Guoji Zhanwang* (World Outlook), Shanghai (October 23, 1995): 3–4.

Chen, Qimao. "New Approaches in China's Foreign Policy: The Post-Cold War Era." *Asian Survey* 37, No. 3 (March 1993): 237–251.

Chinworth, Michael. *Inside Japan's Defense.* London: Brassey's, Inc., 1992.

Chiu, Hungdah. "Constitutional Development and Reform in the Republic of China on Taiwan." In *Contemporary China and the Changing International Community,* edited by B. Lin, and J. Myers, 3–34. South Carolina: University of South Carolina Press, 1994.

Christensen, Raymond. "Electoral Reform in Japan." *Asian Survey* 34, No. 7 (July 1994): 589–605.

Claude, Inis. *Power and International Relations.* New York: Random House, 1962.

Clough, R. *Reaching Across The Taiwan Strait.* Boulder: Westview Press, 1993.

Cloughley, Brian. "Japan Ponders Power Projection." *Jane's International Defense Review* 29 (July 1, 1996): 27–30.

Cohen, William. "America's Asia-Pacific Security Strategy." *Defense Issues* 13, No. 9 (January 1998): 1–5.

———. "Working Together Is Best Avenue for U.S. and China." *Defense Issues* 13, No. 12 (January 1998): 1–4.

Cole, Bernard. "Asia at Sea." *U.S. Naval Institute Proceedings* (March 1997), 36–39.

Cronin, Patrick, and Michael Green. McNair Paper No. 31. *Redefining the U.S.-Japan Alliance: Tokyo's National Defense Program.* Washington, D.C.: National Defense University Press, 1994.

Da Jun. "Where Will Japan Go?" FBIS-CHI (December 7, 1995): 4–5.

Dam, Kenneth, John Deutch, Joseph Nye, and David Rowe. "Harnessing Japan: A U.S. Strategy for Managing Japan's Rise as a Global Power." *Washington Quarterly* 16, No. 2 (Spring 1993): 29–42.

Department of Defense. *United States Security Strategy for the East Asia-Pacific Region.* Washington, D.C.: Office of International Security Affairs, Department of Defense, 1995.

Dittmer, Lowell. "The Strategic Triangle: An Elementary Game-Theoretical Analysis." In *Power, Strategy, and Security,* edited by Klaus Knorr, 37–67. Princeton: Princeton University Press, 1983.

Donnelly, Michael. "On Political Negotiation: America Pushes to Open Up Japan." *Pacific Affairs* 66, No. 3 (Fall 1993): 329–350.

Eto, Jun. "The Japanese Constitution and the Post-Cold War World." *Japan Echo* 18, No. 3 (1991): 62–68.

Feng, Tejun, ed. *Dangdai Shijie Zhengzhijingji Yu Guojiguanxi* (Contemporary World Political Economy and International Relations). Beijing: People's University Press, 1994.

Foreign Broadcast Information Service-China (FBIS-CHI).

Foreign Broadcast Information Service-East Asia (FBIS-EAS).

Foreign Broadcast Information Service-Japan Science & Technology (FBIS-JST).

Foreign Broadcast Information Service-Trends (FBIS-Trends).

Freeman, Chas. "Sino-American Relations: Back to the Basics." *Foreign Policy,* No. 104 (Fall 1996): 3–17.

Freeman, Chas, Harvey Feldman, Harry Harding, and Richard Solomon. "The United States and China Into the 21st Century." An Asian Studies Center Symposium, The Heritage Foundation, Washington, D.C., November 21, 1995.

Friedman, George, and Meredith LeBard. *The Coming War with Japan.* New York: St. Martin's Press, 1991.

Fukushima, Kiyohiko. "The Revival of 'Big Politics' in Japan." *International Affairs* 72, No. 1 (1996): 53–72.

Fukuyama, Francis, and Kongdan Oh. *The U.S.-Japan Security Relationship after the Cold War.* Santa Monica: The RAND, 1993.

Funabashi, Yoichi. "The Asianization of Asia." *Foreign Affairs* 72, No. 5 (1993): 75–85.

Garrett, Banning, and Bonnie Glaser. "Revision of the U.S.-Japan Alliance and Emerging Sino-Japanese Rivalry." Washington, D.C., (1996): 1–27.

Garver, John. "The PLA as an Interest Group in Chinese Foreign Policy." In *Chinese Military Modernization,* edited by Dennison Lane, Mark Weisenbloom, and Dimon Liu, 246–281. Washington, D.C.: AEI Press, 1996.

Ge, Gengfu. "Changes in the Development of Japan's Defense Policy and Defense Capabilities," *Guoji Wenti Yanjiu* (January 1989), 6–12.

George, Alexander. "The Operational Code: A Neglected Approach to the Study of Political Leaders and Decision-Making." *International Studies Quarterly* 13, No. 2 (1969): 190–222.

———. "The Causal Nexus Between Cognitive Beliefs and Decision Making Behavior: The Operational Code." In *Psychological Models in International Politics,* edited by L. Falkowski, 95–124.Boulder: Westview Press, 1979.

Gibert, S., and W. Carpenter, eds. *American and Island China: A Documentary History.* Lanham: University Press of America, 1989.

Gill, Bates, and Taeho Kim. *China's Arms Acquisitions From Abroad.* Oxford: Oxford University Press, 1995.

Gilpin, Robert. *War and Change in World Politics.* Cambridge: Cambridge University Press, 1981.

Goldstein, Joshua, and John Freeman. *Three-Way Street.* Chicago: The University of Chicago Press, 1990.

Gourevitch, Peter. "The Second Image Revisited: International Sources of Domestic Politics." *International Organization* 32, No. 4 (1978): 881–911.

Green, Michael. *Arming Japan.* New York: Columbia University Press, 1995.

Green, Michael J., and Benjamin L. Self. "Japan's Changing China Policy: From Commercial Liberalism to Reluctant Realism." *Survival* 38, No. 2 (1996): 35–58.

Haas, Ernst. "The Balance of Power: Prescription, Concept or Propaganda?" *World Politics* 5, No. 4 (1953): 442–477.

Hagan, Joe. *Political Opposition and Foreign Policy in Comparative Perspective.* Boulder: Lynne Rienner Publishers, 1993.

———. "Domestic Political Systems and War Proneness," *Mershon International Studies Review* 38, No. 2 (1994): 183–207.

Han, Gaorun, and Song Zhongyue. *Dongya Heping Yu Hezuo (East Asian Peace and Cooperation).* Beijing: National Defense University Press, 1994.

Hashimoto, Ryutaro. *Vision of Japan: A Realistic Direction for the 21st Century.* Tokyo: KK Best Sellers, 1994.

Heginbotham, Eric, and Richard Samuels. "Mercantile Realism and Japanese Foreign Policy." *International Security* 22, No. 4 (Spring 1998): 171–203.

Hermann, Margaret, and Charles Hermann. "Who Makes Foreign Policy Decisions and How: An Empirical Inquiry." *International Studies Quarterly* 33, No. 4 (1989): 361–387.

Herrmann, Richard. "The Empirical Challenge of the Cognitive Revolution: A Strategy for Drawing Inferences about Perceptions." *International Studies Quarterly* 32, No. 2 (1988): 175–203.

Hiramatsu, Shigeo. "Chinese Naval Force and the Revival of 'Sinocentrism.'" *The Journal of National Defense* (Shin Boei Ronshu) 20, No. 3 (1992): 22–42.

Hironaka, Yuken. "On the Security of East Asia and the Pacific Region." *The Journal of National Defense* (Shin Boei Ronshu) 21, No.4 (1994): 1–10.

Holsti, Ole, and James Rosenau. "Liberals, Populists, Libertarians, and Conservatives: The Link between Domestic and International Affairs." *International Political Science Review* 17, No. 1 (1996): 29–54.

Holsti, Ole, P. T. Hopmann, and J. D. Sullivan. *Unity and Disintegration in International Alliances: Comparative Studies.* New York: Wiley, 1973.

Horner, Charles. "The Third Side of the Triangle: the China-Japan Dimension" *National Interest* No. 46 (Winter 1996/97): 23–31.

Hosokawa, Morihiro. "Are U.S. Troops in Japan Needed?" *Foreign Affairs* 77, No. 4 (July/August 1998): 2–5.

Hsiung, James. "Sino-U.S.-Soviet Relations in a Triadic-Game Perspective." In *Beyond China's Independent Foreign Policy,* edited by James Hsiung, 107–131. New York: Praeger, 1985.

Huang, Suan. "U.S.-Japanese Contention for Economic Power." *Guoji Wenti Yanjiu* (July 1990): 37–44.

Huang, Zhilian. "Japan's Asia-Pacific Policy toward Twenty-first Century." In *Asia-Pacific Economic Cooperation in the 1990s,* edited by Xitang Yao and Qimao Chen, 1122–1135. Shanghai: Shanghai Social Sciences Academy, 1990.

Ianaka, Akihiko. "Japan's Security Policy in the 1990s." In *Japan's International Agenda,* edited by Funabashi, 28–56. NY: New York University Press, 1994.

Ijiri, Hidenori. "Sino-Japanese Controversy Since the 1972 Diplomatic Normalization." *China Quarterly* No. 124 (December 1990): 639–661.

Inoguchi, Takashi. "Distant Neighbors? Japan and Asia." *Current History* 94, No. 595 (November 1995): 392–396.

Institute for National Strategic Studies (INSS). *Strategic Assessment 1995.* Washington, D.C.: National Defense University Press, 1995.

International Institute for Strategic Studies. *The Military Balance 1995–1996.* London: Oxford University Press, 1995.

Iriye, Akira. "Chinese-Japanese Relations, 1945–90." *China Quarterly,* No. 124 (December 1990): 624–638.

Ishihara, Shintaro. *The Japan That Can Say No.* Translated by Frank Baldwin. New York: Simon & Schuster, 1991.

Iwata, Ryushi. "Advancement in a Schooling-Conscious Society." *Japan Echo* 6, No. 4 (1979): 18–28.

Japan Defense Agency (JDA). *Defense of Japan.* Tokyo: JDA, 1994, 1995, 1996, 1997.

Jervis, Robert. *Perception and Misperception in International Politics.* Princeton: Princeton University Press, 1976.

Johnson, Chalmers. "Containing China: U.S. and Japan Drift Toward Disaster." *Japan Quarterly* 43, No. 4 (October-December 1996): 10–18.

Johnson, Chalmers, and E. B. Keehn. "The Pentagon's Ossified Strategy." *Foreign Affairs* 74, No. 4 (July/August 1995): 103–115.

Kacowicz, A. "The Problem of Peaceful Territorial Change." *International Studies Quarterly* 38, No. 2 (1994): 219–254.

Karniol, Robert. "Northeast Asia: A Changing Region." *Jane's Defense '96: The World in Conflict* (1996): 52.

Kasahara, Masaaki. "China's New Security Concept." *The Journal of National Defense* (Shin Boei Ronshu) 18, No. 3 (1990): 44–59.

———. "Japan-U.S. Relationship and China Problem." *The Journal of National Defense* (Shin Boei Ronshu) 19, No. 4 (1992): 18–26.

———. "The Security of Asia in the Near Future." *The Journal of National Defense* (Shin Boei Ronshu) 21, No. 4 (1994): 11–18.

Katzenstein, Peter. "International Relations and Domestic Structures." In *Between Power and Plenty,* edited by Peter Katzenstein, 3–22. Madison: University of Wisconsin Press, 1978.

Katzenstein, Peter, and Nobuo Okawara. "Japan's National Security." *International Security* 17, No. 4 (Spring 1993a): 84–118.

———. *Japan's National Security.* Ithaca: Cornell University Press, 1993b.

Kawasaki, Tsuyoshi. "Structural Transformation in the U.S.-Japanese Economic Relationship." In *Power, Economics, and Security: The United States and Japan in Focus,* edited by Henry Bienen, 266–285. Boulder: Westview Press, 1992.

Keddell, Joseph. *The Politics of Defense in Japan.* Armonk, NY: M. E. Sharpe, 1993.

Kegley, Charles, and Gregory Raymond. "Must We fear a Post-Cold War Multipolar System." *Journal of Conflict Resolution* 36, No. 3 (September 1992): 573–585.

Kenjiro, Hayashi. "Passing the Torch of World Leadership." *Japan Echo* 7, No. 4 (1985): 8–14.

Kim, Ilpyong, ed. *The Strategic Triangle: China, the United States and the Soviet Union.* New York: Paragon House Publishers, 1987.

Klintworth, Gary. "The Chinese Navy to Get Some Big Guns, at Last." *Asia-Pacific Defense Reporter* (April-May 1997): 6–7.

Krasner, Stephen. *Defending the National Interest: Raw Materials Investment and U.S. Foreign Policy.* Princeton: Princeton University Press, 1978.

Kugler, Richard. *U.S. Military Strategy and Force Posture for the 21st Century.* Santa Monica: The RAND, 1994.

Lake, D. A. "Powerful Pacifists: Democratic States and War." *American Political Science Review* 86, No. 1 (1992): 24–37.

Lamborn, Alan. *The Price of Power.* Boston: Unwin and Hyman, 1991.

Lasater, Martin. "Growing U.S. Interests in the New Taiwan." *Orbis* 37, No. 2 (Spring 1993): 239–258.

Layne, Christopher. "Less is More: Minimal Realism in East Asia." *The National Interest.* No. 43 (Spring 1996): 64–77.

———. "A House of Cards: American Strategy toward China." *World Policy Journal* 14, No. 3 (Fall 1997): 77–98.

Levin, Norman. "Prospects for U.S.-Japanese Security Cooperation." In *Japan's*

Emerging Global Power, edited by Danny Unger and Paul Blackburn, 71–84. Boulder: Lynne Rienner Publishers, 1993.

Levin, Norman, Mark Lorell, and Arthur Alexander. *The Wary Warriors: Future Directions in Japanese Security Policies.* Santa Monica: The RAND, 1993.

Levy, Jack. "The Diversionary Theory of War: A Critique." In *Handbook of War Studies,* edited by Manus Midlarsky, 259–288. Boston: Unwin Hyman, 1989.

Liao, Xinan, and Sang Zhonglin. "A Potential Nuclear Power: Japan." *Bingqi Zhishi (Ordnance Knowledge)* (November 1995): 14–15.

Lieberthal, Kenneth. "Domestic Forces and Sino-U.S. Relations." In *Living With China,* edited by Ezra Vogel, 254–276. New York: W.W. Norton & Company, 1997.

Lin, Chong-pin. "The Military Balance in the Taiwan Straits." *China Quarterly,* No. 146 (June 1996): 577–595.

Lin, Daizhao. *Zhanhou Zhongri Guanxishi* (The Postwar Sino-Japanese Relations, 1945–1992). Beijing: Beijing University Press, 1992.

Lincoln, Edward. *Japan's New Global Role.* Washington, D.C.: Brookings Institution, 1993.

Lord, Winston. "The United States and the Security of Taiwan." *U.S. Department of State Dispatch* (March 25, 1996): 151–154.

Lorell, Mark. *Troubled Partnership: A History of U.S.-Japan Collaboration on the FS-X Fighter.* Santa Monica: The RAND, 1995.

Mahbubani, Kishore. "An Asia-Pacific Consensus." *Foreign Affairs* 76, No. 5 (September/October 1997): 149–158.

Manning, Robert. "Futureshock or Renewed Partnership? The U.S.-Japan Alliance Facing the Millennium." *Washington Quarterly* 18, No. 4 (Autumn 1995): 87–98.

Medvedev, Roy. *China and the Superpowers.* Translated by Harold Shukman. New York: Basil Blackwell, 1986.

Mendl, Wolf. *Issues in Japan's China Policy.* New York: Oxford University Press, 1978.

Mochizuki, Mike. "A New Bargain for a Stronger Alliance." In *Toward a True Alliance: Restructuring U.S.-Japan Security Relations,* edited by Mochizuki, 5–42. Washington, D.C.: Brookings Institution Press, 1997.

MOFA. *National Defense Program Outline in and after FY 1996.* Internet Service, (December 1995).

Montaperto, Ronald. "Reality Check: Assessing the Chinese Military Threat." *Defense Working Group Policy Brief.* (February 1998): 1–20.

Montaperto, Ronald, and Karl Eikenberry. "Paper Tiger: a Skeptical Appraisal of China's Military Might." *Harvard International Review* 18, No. 2 (Spring 1996): 28–31.

Morimoto, Satoshi. "The Security Environment in East Asia," In *Toward A True Alliance: Restructuring U.S.-Japan Security Relations,* edited by Mike

Mochizuki, 83–95. Washington, D.C.: Brookings Institution Press, 1997.

Munro, Ross. "Giving Taipei a Place at the Table." *Foreign Affairs* 73, No. 6 (Nov./Dec. 1994a): 109–122.

———. "Eavesdropping on the Chinese Military: Where It Expects War—Where It Doesn't." *Orbis* 38, No. 3 (Summer 1994 b): 355–372.

National Development Conference Secretariat. *National Development Conference Resolutions* (Taipei: 1997).

Ni, Feng. "Clinton Seeks Closer Security Ties with Japan." *Beijing Review* (May 6–12, 1996): 8–9.

Nishi, Masanori. "Japan's Defense Strategy." Washington, D.C: Atlantic Council of the United States, 1996, 1–61.

Nishihara, Masashi. "Northeast Asia and Japanese Security." In *Japan's Emerging Global Role,* edited by Danny Unger and Paul Blackburn, 85–98. Boulder: Lynne Rienner Publishers, 1993.

———. "Japan's Receptivity to Conditional Engagement." In *Weaving the Net: Conditional Engagement with China,* edited by James Shinn, 175–190. New York: Council on Foreign Relations Press, 1996.

Norris, Robert, Andrew Burrows, and Richard Fieldhouse, eds. *Nuclear Weapons Databook,* Vol. V, *British, French, and Chinese Nuclear Weapons.* Boulder: Westview Press, 1994.

Numata, Sadaaki. "Japan: Toward a More Active Political and Security Role?" *RUSI Journal* (June 1996): 11–14.

Nye, Joseph. "The Case for Deep Engagement." *Foreign Affairs* 74, No. 4 (July/August 1995): 90–102.

O'Hanlon, Michael. "Theater Missile Defense and the U.S.-Japan Alliance." In *Toward a True Alliance,* edited by Mike Mochizuki, 179–192. Washington, D.C.: Brookings Institution Press, 1997.

Oshima, Kenzo. "Japan's Relations with the United States: Issues and Prospects." *Journal of Northeast Asian Studies* 6, No. 2, 1992: 57–64.

Ozawa, Ichiro. *Blueprint for a New Japan.* Tokyo: Kodansha International, 1994.

Panel on Sino-US Relations toward the 21st Century. "Trends of Future Sino-US Relations and Policy Proposals." Beijing, (September 1994): 1–28.

Perry, William. Speech at the National Defense University, Washington, D.C., February 13, 1996.

Porteous, Holly. "China's View of Strategic Weapons." *Jane's Intelligence Review* 29 (March 1996): 134–137.

Putnam, Robert. "Diplomacy and Domestic Politics: The Logic of Two Level Games." *International Organization* 42, No. 3 (1988): 427–460.

Pyle, Kenneth. *The Japanese Question: Power and Purpose in a New Era.* Washington, D.C.: The AEI Press, 1992.

———. "Uncertain Future: Revitalizing the US-Japan Alliance." *Harvard International Review* 18, No. 2 (Spring 1996): 36–37; 73–74.

Rapoport, Anatol. "Introduction." In *Game Theory as a Theory of Conflict Resolution, Dordrecht,* edited by Rapoport, 1–6. Holland: D. Reidel Publishing, 1974.

Robinson, Thomas. "Triple Detente? The Strategic Triangle in the Late Twentieth Century." In *The Gorbachev Generation,* edited by Jane Zacek, 95–124. New York: Paragon House, 1988.

Rong, Zhi. "Major Powers' Military Strategies and Our Own Policy toward the End of This Century." In *Guoji Xingshi yu Guofang Zhanlue* (The International Situation and Defense Strategy). Beijing: The Academy of Military Sciences Press, 1987, 67–73.

Rosecrance, Richard, and Arthur A. Stein. *The Domestic Bases of Grand Strategy.* Ithaca: Cornell University Press, 1993.

Ross, Robert, ed. *China, the United States, and the Soviet Union.* Armonk, NY: M.E. Sharpe, 1993.

Ross, Robert. *Managing a Changing Relationship: China's Japan Policy in the 1990s.* Carlisle Barracks, PA: U.S. Army War College, 1996.

Roy, Denny. "Hegemon on the Horizon?—China's Threat to East Asian Security." *International Security* 19, No. 1 (Summer 1994): 149–168.

Rummel, R. J. "Libertarianism and International Violence." *Journal of Conflict Resolution* 27, No. 1 (1983): pp. 27–71.

SAIS. *The United States and Japan in 1996: Redefining the Partnership.* Washington, D.C.: Johns Hopkins University, 1996.

Samuels, Richard. *"Rich Nation, Strong Army:" National Security and the Technological Transformation of Japan.* Ithaca: Cornell University Press, 1994.

Sarkesian, Sam. *U.S. National Security.* Boulder: Lynne Rienner Publishers, 1995.

Sasae, Kenichiro. *Rethinking Japan-US Relations.* Adelphi Paper 292. London: International Institute for Strategic Studies, 1994.

Sato, Seizaburo. "Japanese Perceptions of the New Security Situation." In *The Collapse of the Soviet Empire: Managing the Regional Fallout,* edited by T. Taylor, 171–189. London: Royal Institute of International Affairs, 1992.

———. "Clarifying the Right of Collective Self-Defense." *Asia-Pacific Review* 3 (Fall-Winter 1996): 91–105.

Sato, Seizaburo, Shumpei Kumon, and Yasusuke Murakami. "Analysis of Japan's Modernization." *Japan Echo* 3, No. 3 (1976): 72–91.

Satoh, Yukio. "Emerging Trends in Asia-Pacific Security: The Role of Japan." *The Pacific Review* 8, No. 2 (1995): 267–281.

Schelling, Thomas. *The Strategy of Conflict.* New York: Oxford University Press, 1963.

Segal, Gerald. *The Great Power Triangle.* New York: St. Martin's Press, 1982.

———. "China's Changing Shape." *Foreign Affairs* 73, No. 3 (May/June 1994): 43–58.

Shambaugh, David. "The United States and China: A New Cold War?" *Current History* 94, No. 593 (September 1995): 241–247.

———. "Taiwan's Security: Maintaining Deterrence Amid Political Accountability." *China Quarterly,* No. 148 (December 1996): 1284–1318.

Sing, Lam Lai. "A Short Note on ASEAN-Great Power Interaction." *Contemporary Southeast Asia* 15, No. 4 (March 1994): 451–463.

Snyder, Glenn, and Paul Diesing. *Conflict among Nations.* Princeton, Princeton University Press, 1977.

Snyder, Jack. *Myths of Empire: Domestic Politics and International Ambition.* Ithaca: Cornell University Press, 1991.

Song, Qiang, Zhang Zangzang, and Qiao Bian. *Zhongguo Keyi Shuo Bu* (The China That Can Say No). Beijing: Zhonghua Gongshang Lianhe Chubanshe, 1996.

Stuart, Douglas, and William Tow. Adelphi Paper No. 299. *A US Strategy for the Asia-Pacific.* London: IISS/Oxford University Press, 1995.

Sutter, Robert. "Taiwan: Recent Developments and U.S. Policy Choices." *CRS Issues Brief* (March 26, 1994a): 1–13.

———. "Cross-Strait Relations and their Implications for the United States." *Issues and Studies* (December 1994b): 1–15.

———. "East Asia: The New Triangular Relationship, Implications for U.S. Influence, and Options for U.S. Policy." *CRS Report for Congress,* 94–463S (May 31, 1994c): 1–6.

Takahashi, Takuma. "Economic Interdependence and Security in the East Asia-Pacific Region." In *Toward a True Alliance: Restructuring U.S.-Japan Security Relations,* edited by Mike Mochizuki, 96–136. Washington, D.C.: Brookings Institution Press, 1997.

Tamamoto, Masaru. "Japan's Search for a World Role." In *Power, Economics, and Security: The United States and Japan in Focus,* edited by Henry Bienen, 226–253. Boulder: Westview Press, 1992.

———. "The Japan That Wants to be Liked: Society and International Participation." In *Japan's Emerging Global Role,* edited by Danny Unger and Paul Blackburn, 37–54. Boulder: Lynne Rienner Publishers, 1993.

Tsukamoto, Katsuichi. "Military Situation in Far East and Aspects of Threats." *The Journal of National Defense* (Shin Boei Ronshu) 18, No. 2 (1990): 31–40.

U.S. Department of Defense. *A Strategic Framework for the Asian Pacific Rim: Looking toward the 21st Century,* April 1990.

———. *A Strategic Framework for the Asian Pacific Rim: Report to Congress 1992,* April 1992.

U.S. Government. "Joint Communique on the Establishment of Diplomatic Relations Between the United States and the People's Republic of China," *Public Papers of the Presidents of the United States: Jimmy Carter 1978,* II (December 15, 1978): 2264–2266.

Unger, Danny. "The Problem of Global Leadership: Waiting for Japan." In *Japan's Emerging Global Role,* edited by Danny Unger and Paul Blackburn, 3–20. Boulder: Lynne Rienner Publishers, 1993.

Vasquez, John. *The War Puzzle.* Cambridge: Cambridge University Press, 1993.

Waltz, Kenneth. *Theory of International Politics.* Reading: Wiley and Addision, 1979.

White House. "A National Security Strategy of Engagement and Enlargement." (Washington, D.C.: U.S. Government Printing Office, July 1994): 1–29.

Wilson, Ian. "Sino-Japanese Relations in the Post-Cold War World." In *China as a Great Power,* edited by Stuart Harris and Gary Klintworth, 91–106. New York: St. Martin's Press, 1995.

Yamazaki, Takio. "U.S. Foreign Policy in View of the Japanese-American-Chinese Triangular Relationship." *Jiyu,* No. 444 (February 1997): 69–75.

Yi, Xiaoxiong. "China's U.S. Policy Conundrum in the 1990s." *Asian Survey* 34, No. 8 (August 1994): 675–691.

Zeringue, Marshal, and Daniel Kritenbrink. "Japanese Security Policy in a Changing International Environment." *Defense Analysis* 10, No. 2 (1994): 113–140.

Zhan, Jun. "The Development of the 'Soft-ware' in the Mainland's Military Forces" (Dalu Junshi Liliang 'Ruanjian' de Fazhan). (Paper presented at the conference "Military Conflicts over the Taiwan Strait," Los Angeles, December 1994): 130–137.

Zhang, Dalin. "RiMei Tongweng Xiang Hechuqu?" (Where Will the Japan-U.S. Alliance Go?). *Guoji Wenti Yanjiu* (International Studies) (January 1996): 26–30.

Zhang, Ming. *Dui Ri Gouhe Yu Meiguo Anquan Zhengce* (Peace Settlement with Japan and American Security Policy). (Master's Thesis, Nanjing University, 1986).

———. *Major Powers at a Crossroads: Economic Interdependence and an Asia Pacific Security Community.* Boulder: Lynne Rienner Publishers, 1995.

———. "The New Thinking of Sino-U.S. Relations: An Interview Note," *Journal of Contemporary China* 6, No. 14 (Spring 1997): 117–123.

———. "The Role of the PLA in Nonproliferation and Arms Control Decision-making." (Paper presented at the conference, "Individuals, Institutions, and Policies in the Chinese Nonproliferation and Arms Control Community," Monterey, California, November 1997): 1–11.

Zheng, Shi. "Riben—Qianzai de He Daodan Daguo" (Japan—A Potential Great Nuclear Missile Power). *Jing Bao* (Mirror monthly), (November 1996): 74–77.

Zheng, Zhiren. "Woguo Zhoubian Guojia he Diqu de Dididaodan" (The Development of Surface-to-Surface Missiles in the Countries around China). *Bingqi Zhishi* (Ordnance Knowledge) (May 1996): 5–8.

Zhou, Jihua. "Japan's Foreign Policy Choices for the Twenty-first Century: A Chinese Perspective." In *Japan in the Posthegemonic World,* edited by Tsuneo Akaha and Frank Langon, 185–200. Boulder: Lynne Rienner Publishers, 1993.

Zhu, Hongqian. "China and the Triangular Relationship," In *The Chinese View of the World,* edited by Yufan Hao and Guocang Huan, 31–56. New York: Pantheon Books, 1989.

Zhu, Qizhen. "Queli Mianxiang Ershiyi Shiji de Zhong Ri Mei Hezuo Guanxi" (Sino-U.S.-Japanese Cooperative Relationship Facing the 21st Century). *Peace and Development,* Total No. 51, No. 1 (1995): 10–12.

Zi, Shui, and Xiao Shi. *Jingti Riben Junguo Zhuyi* (Vigilant Against Japanese Militarism). Beijing: Jincheng Press, 1997.

Zinnes, D. A. "Why War? Evidence of the Outbreak of International Conflict." In *Handbook of Political Conflict,* edited by T. R. Gurr, 331–360. New York: Free Press, 1980.

Zoellick, Robert. "China: What Engagement Should Mean." *National Interest,* No. 46 (Winter 1996/97): 13–22.

Index